THIS SIDE
OF THE PAST

Volume II

THIS SIDE
OF THE PAST

Volume II

Dick and The Mission Girls

DORIS
HAGEDORN

XULON PRESS ELITE

Xulon Press Elite
2301 Lucien Way #415
Maitland, FL 32751
407.339.4217
www.xulonpress.com

Printed in the United States of America.

ISBN-13: 978-1-54566-571-8

ACKNOWLEDGEMENTS

Thanks and appreciation to Dick Proeneke and his family who so graciously shared their lives with all who read Dick's books. We consider this Dick's Book as well!

Thanks and appreciation to our friends, Jeff and Cheryl Disney and Matt and Cheryl Gebhardt who were "such a great help when we needed honest advice and computer help!"

Thanks and appreciation to Artist Jeff Disney, who's skill—and a devoted heart for God—inspires more books! We look forward to the next cover painting—and future collection.

Thanks and appreciation to Katherine Meyers and John Branson of National Park Service for their help, and for the privilege of using selected pictures from Dick's fine collection. (See page 185 for further acknowledgements.)

There are few people in this world who leave such a variety of indelible impressions on others as Richard L. "Dick" Proenneke. With insatiable curiosity and disciplined order, Dick approached nearly everything with vigor; his physical stamina was legendary, his mental prowess remarkable. The word *"can't"* was most likely applied to *failure*. His formula for success seemed to be serious evaluation, contemplation of consequences—and hard work.

Dick had an inquisitive mind, and his appreciation for the creation that surrounded him at Twin Lakes produced some incredible footage—observations of which we are beneficiaries. Facts were very important to Dick, for without them, where would he find sane conclusions—or solutions?

What roll could *"faith"* play in Dick's experience? One of my last great conversations with Dick was regarding his time at Twin Lakes. I posed this question: "If you were to live it all over again, what would you do differently?" His reply: "I would have spent more time with people in some way rather than isolating myself to selfishly enjoy what I wanted to do." He wanted more opportunity, it seemed, for a greater lasting influence.

Perhaps the Mission Girls had more of an influence on Dick than we realized? Or perhaps Dick had more of an influence on the world of mankind than he realized? We know his work will continue to inspire future generations, and we know our Great Creator and the Holy Scriptures of the Bible bring wisdom and insight to the seeking heart.

The communications that appear in this delightful manuscript will give you a new appreciation for a less known and celebrated side of this remarkable man we all knew and appreciated here at Lake Clark—Dick Proenneke.

Endorsement: Glen Alsworth

Dick Proenneke was quick to write letters—even to us, addressing the envelopes to the Mission Girls. We—among many—were blessed with his friendship.

Dick's cabin home at Twin Lakes

"…without faith it is impossible to please Him, for he who comes to God must believe that He is, and that He is a rewarder of those who diligently seek Him." Heb. 11:6

Twin Lakes
April 29, 1975

Dear Florence and Doris,

Thank you both for the nice letters which I received last mail call, April 13th. Next mail delivery will be May 4th which is my birthday. Won't that be a treat? Babe said last time, the 13th, "My birthday is today." Birthday flights one after the other!

Good to hear that both of you are in good health and planning for the trip back to Alaska. And again, it was the best news ever, Doris, that your mother is making good progress. The warm days of spring will hasten her recovery. Here today, temperature is forty-two degrees with a nice breeze from the high mountains. Snow is soft and melting, but it is still about thirty inches deep. Thirty-seven inches of ice on the lake as of April 1, and a good snow cover. No bare ground or gravel showing on any of the creek or river flats—so no wild flowers yet. It won't be too long before they show on the south slope of the mountain across the lake. At the base of the huge rock face near the water fall is a good place to view the first ones. The rocks act as reflectors, warming the soil early.

Guess what! One of my bears came out and I am watching the other den closely. The first one went into the den October 10 and was in 192 days. Much loafing about the den entrance for a few hours, but after that it was a big run on the mountain slope — back and forth, up and down he went!

I wonder if it was to get in shape after the long rest. About a half hour of such activity and he climbed to the base of a rock out-crop and stretched out — feet to the mountain, back to the sun — for that long noon-time nap that the bear enjoys so much. This second bear is now nine days later in coming out, and they say a mother with a new cub or cubs may be as much as a month later in coming out. So, I am hoping for some cubs! Strange that there was little attempt to dig for roots, but he did eat a little snow to quench his thirst.

The Park Service film has 14,500 feet exposed with 600 to go. I want to get a copy of the edited film, and if I do, I guess you know we will have a show! I have a tame cow and calf moose that you would like. The second time I saw them she decided I was no threat. She shows no fear—even at less than a hundred feet—and the calf does as his mom does! I saw them yesterday for the first time in about three weeks. They knew me, I was sure of it for they didn't show the least bit of fear. Both lost much weight in the last month, and I will be glad when the snow melts down to make travel easier for them. They move very little in daytime, and are now peeling the bark from the willows for food—along with their ration of twigs. Sincerely, Dick

Sorry to disappoint you about going to Port Alsworth via the long trail. Had there been someone here to keep my perishables from freezing, I am sure that I would have gone. I had about six dozen eggs, many potatoes and green vegetables. Temperatures were running as low as minus 15 with five readings from zero on down. The snow hadn't settled then, but now a good crust in freezing weather. A day like today would make it soft and wet—tough going—and hard on snowshoes. I have been to Lachbuna Lake on the Kijik, and that is about half way and the toughest half. Once on the lake it would be a breeze.

Sis writes that her dad talks a lot about Hawaii—and moving there. He told me, "There are so many Alaskans over there; I suspect they don't like to see

7

more come, but I guess if one just went there to live, they wouldn't mind too much." I think that he—and Mary too—would miss Lake Clark, in particular, and Alaska in general. Lots of friends—and I'm thinking they would get a little homesick for a good snow-storm, the garden, the goats and all the friends they know that drop in occasionally. When Mary first mentioned it, he says "I haven't seen all of *Alaska* yet!"

I am sure you two would enjoy a trip north by ferry should the weather be nice. I have made the trip from Prince Rupert a couple times. Haines was my getting-off place of course. The first trip went to Sitka—which is a treat—and if you would like to visit Sitka for a little while, you might investigate the schedule and see which ferry to take.

Terry and Vic wanted to be in the hills by May 1st—the last I heard from Terry. They had talked April 1st, but on flying over, Terry and Bill Johnson found four feet of snow in the creek bottom where the cabin is. There has been very little melting. Terry's Vic is a good and faithful wife to go back year after year, but she seems to enjoy it as much as he.

I'll close for now. Thanks again for writing, and thank you for remembering me with the leaflets and your art work—very nice I think. And to your mother, "Get well soon so you can visit Nondalton again, and it would be nice if you could come with the mission girls to Twin Lakes when they come—*and they had better*." Have a good and safe trip cross-country and *north to the future*. Sincerely, Dick

May 3, and it is twins for my number two bear that went in last October 28. She came out yesterday morning, but only for twenty minutes the first time—then she backed into the den again. I could see cubs romping about inside, and later they came to the entrance. They were very dark little guys, and she—the old mother—is a very large and dark bear. Now comes that two years of constant supervision to give those little guys the best education possible—before she says "get going, you are on your own now." I was there when she showed up to greet the cubs—now four months old. R.L.P.

From Flo and Doris to Dick: 1975

The blueberries are nearly gone; the cranberries are ready to harvest. We've canned several jars of sauce, and have a few bags of berries in the freezer—along with moose and caribou. It is nice to have that little freezer!

It was special to see our families—They always welcome us with open arms, and give us a place to anchor. Doris' Mom had her surgery, in July of '74 and by March of '75 up to 79 lbs. Doctor's diagnosis was pernicious anemia. She endured the pain and the mean iron and B12 shots, though it was hard on Doris (me) to give them!! I stayed with Mom (WA) until the end of May then flew United Airlines to spend three weeks with Flo and family (MI), after which we drove the car across to WA and caught the ferry from Prince Rupert to Haines, AK. It was always hard to leave our families. We would get up the road a safe distance, then burst into sobs and tears! Thankfully, Mom had a good report from her Doctors, and was up to 96 lbs. by the time we left. How we thank God for his love, mercy and care! The ride from Prince Rupert was special; very beautiful and rewarding; wish Mom had been able to come with us! Flo's Mom would have enjoyed the trip as well, but she had gone "Home to Heaven" a few years before.

Allen's wife Barbara writes of their visit to Nondalton in June, 1978: Allen had the opportunity to fly with Babe to Dick's cabin. They delivered the mail and supplies. Allen remembered hanging on real tight when landing on the water. It was a new experience for Allen; first time on floats. He said Babe would glance at him and smile as he, Allen, grabbed the dash and tubing in front of him. Allen also learned of Allen Mountain! I think you, Dick, told him! Thanks

TWIN LAKES
APRIL 4, 1980

Dear Florence and Doris,

Now at 5:30 PM a beautiful afternoon. It has been snowing most all day, and really putting it down the past couple hours—then nothing but blue sky and bright sun.

Thank you for your good letter of way back, January 30, Florence. In it you wrote of the dark and the cold and keeping things working. Late March and early April is nice for those who say winter is nicer than summer. Here at the lakes, all of the snow and ice are here, and snow still comes, but the sun is high and warm and camera gear—and me—performs more efficiently at 25 to 35 degrees.

I left my two sisters healthy and happy in Iowa. Helen insists that she has made her last move. This is it—she likes it in Donnellson after Chicago since 1936. For my part, I wouldn't care to be reminded that the nursing home where my other sister Florence works is only a half mile away. I visited some old timers there and thought it was sad. I wouldn't enjoy working there as Florence does and be constantly reminded that all too soon I may be a resident—waiting!

On leaving Iowa, I took Amtrack to L.A. My brother Raymond and I flew United to Spokane to see Spike and Hope C. I am happy to say they both appeared in good health. Raymond went back, and I went on to Seattle and up. A few days in Anchorage, and then out with Glen and two others from Port Alsworth area—Frank E. and Tony B. from across the lake I think—I enjoyed my one full day there, and nearly made it to Nondalton. Glen was flying the Victory High team there and mentioned if he had room I was welcome to go—but no room. Maybe some time it will work out. At the price of gas these days, one watches his chasing around.

We came in March 24th to find it just like winter— but the sun and temperature high. No sign of any great amount of melting. Snow was about forty-two inches in the timber, and ice on the lake twenty-nine inches. It should be out by June 1st. I had a heap of shoveling to do, and I didn't mind, for my cabin was just as I had left it—October 18, 1979. That new indoor-outdoor carpet showed no signs of a bad spill that someone might have had if anyone had stayed awhile. Airplane ski-tracks of different widths were out front, so a couple airplanes had been here. No one had lived in the cabin, I am sure.

Only a couple days here, and a lucky find: On a nest that I discovered last fall was a great horned owl—and incubating! Setting on two eggs—and for how long? I can only guess. Does it seem early for hatching? Camp robbers are very early, but I doubt they are nesting yet. To see her, the great horned owl, on that big, heavily-stacked stick-nest reminds me of a big heavy cat crouched there. Those horns resemble ears of a tufted-eared cat. The horned owl is a shy one—but not when nesting. I have a tall ladder which reaches nearly the level of the nest. From the top—and twenty feet away—I have a perfect shot at her with my 300mm (6x) lens. Those big-yellow-brown-eyes blink slowly, together or alternately, one then the other—something I can't duplicate. Now to watch the young one's hatch and grow! Interesting!

I've seen no moose, and I'm not surprised, with the snow so deep. Did the winter have lots of wind? Above brush line, the mountains are nearly free of snow. I have seen sixteen head of sheep at one time—until now. The lower lake area was wind-swept with sixty head of caribou!

The Park Service paid off in full with duplicate slides and 16mm film. Raymond has both at his apartment. He is set up—and working—putting a film together. I am not sure at what length he will go with the finished product—filter, music and narration? We took some of his rough editing to Spokane for Spike and Hope to see. They thought it good, but to city folks, all film of wilderness is good to view.

It looks like a busy summer and fall ahead. If everyone comes who has threatened to come, I will become a tour guide. Now that this country has become a show place, I would enjoy showing interested people some points of interest that I have discovered in my fourteen years and more of poking around.

Glen won't be in until late April, I suspect, as he, Wayne and families plan on a trip to see Babe and Mary—in Hawaii. What is this I hear about Babe having health problems? He seemed so fit when he and Mary were here last summer. They say he feels it was the flu—and after effects. I hope it was nothing more. I Must close for now, and do hope this finds you both healthy and happy—and your friends and relatives as well. My Best, Dick.

P. S. About the book, I almost forgot. Don't confuse it with the yellow-covered magazine. It's a hard-cover-book "Exploring America's Back Country." The Lake Clark section is written by John Kauffmann, photography by Jim Brandenburg.

April 12th, I don't envy you your messy break-up. It is still real nice here—ten degree, clear and calm the past three mornings, with very little sign of melting. Please ask Ruth, "When do Great Horned Owls hatch?" If she says "about April 10th" she knows just about *everything—as she one time told me she did!* They did hatch two days ago!

April 19th, no little airplanes have stopped for tea. Glen may come next week. Guess what? The bears are out. The old lame one who carried the tiny cub by a hind leg, and the now two-year-old triplets. High on the mountain—and the den close by—I must climb and see just how much room it takes to sleep four for six months and not get cabin fever!

The Great Horned Owl

Twin Lakes
July 24, 1982

Dear Florence and Doris,

Greetings from my very soggy Twin Lakes country! There has been lots of rain the past several days. It has me thinking of the early seventies—and the lake level nine inches below my floor. There's nothing close to that at present. In fact, the lake was higher earlier this summer.

Thanks for the good letter, Florence. It's always good to hear from the mission girls. My correspondent in Redlands, California was happy to get the copy of Arctic Echoes you sent to me. She is seventy-seven and seems a good sort. She writes that she feels you are her kind of people—people she would like to have as friends. She lives next to the city park, so has lots of squirrels and birds as friends. It was good news, and may it always be so, that your medical report was good, Florence.

I haven't seen much of Glen since this past spring. His new pilot drops in with groceries and mail when flying this way. He's a good pilot, too, I suspect. Leon has been along the last couple of trips, and rides the captain's seat in the 206. It seems only a little while since he and Sig were little guys living with you two. Guess you know that Glen has a beautiful new plane now—a Beaver.

Imagine, no more light-plant baby-sitting, and live T.V. to stare at! Nondalton is going big-time. Don't forget the good old days. I subscribed to a popular news magazine for six months—and didn't renew. They had lots of good stuff, but they certainly dramatized the news—even the photo coverage. It seems if they need a certain expression on the person's face, they have it. That's because of the new electric wind and three to five frames per recorded 35mm's. Think of the hundreds and hundreds of pictures taken for everyone used!

Now, no news magazine, and life is more like it used to be. Be ignorant and happy! Someone drops in and I ask them, *"What's new Outside?" (Outside, meaning outside of Twin Lakes area. This term has also been used to mean "outside of Alaska")*

Just a few days ago—and a perfect clear, calm and forty-degree morning—the Park Service flew in Ray Arnett, from D.C. I asked him, "How's it going?" "Oh great!" was his reply. He enjoyed my view out of the big window—for half an hour, I guess. He was very much impressed with "One Man's Wilderness," and promised to send me a new flag to fly—one that was flown over the White House. I hear they want to cut the size of some Parks, and add to the preserves surrounding them—to create more hunting area. I hope they leave Twin Lakes locked up tight. Twin Lakes use to be *heaven*—until August 10th when it came alive with people carrying guns and wanting to kill something. I did get my little XA-2 Olympics camera and like it very much—7.1 oz. and three fingers wide lying in the palm of my hand. It's completely automatic of course, and makes me work pretty hard to keep from being a dumb one. Two days ago, I was changing film here in the cabin—thought I would see the action of the shutter with the back open— very erratic, slow, fast and in-between. I was ready to box it up and send it to the shop. Then it struck me! The light sensor was seeing dim, bright and in-between—giving shutter speeds to suit. Aim it at the window, and it was fast. Under the table it was a two-second exposure. Smart Japanese invention!

Did I tell you that after three hundred miles of exercise, my owl study ended with a broken neck suffered by one of my star actors? I found the owl under the tree. There was no sign of its mate, so I don't know if it flew or was plucked clean by another large predator bird. Once—while I was on watch—a goshawk dived at the nest while mom-owl was still with the owlets. Later, she left the nest to stand guard from a perch as far as fifty to one hundred yards away. The goshawk could easily swoop in and hit them hard with a heavy talon. Now I am filming the *three young goshawks*! They are ready to fly any day now. They are very light on their feet when they exercise those wings. I have been hit a few times by their mom. Once, she snatched my knit watch-cap from my head and flew out of sight with it—through the cottonwoods. I watched, and finally found it at the base of a cottonwood tree. A few days ago, she wasn't home and I was enjoying my freedom of filming without guarding. I was on a ladder, resting my 300mm on a limb—waiting for better light—when *POW*! Something struck my left shoulder from behind. A second later she was on the nest with the kids—then right back at me again. She can get pretty mad! Always before, she would holler as she came at me, but not this time. So it took me by complete surprise. I later learned she had sliced my nylon windbreaker in three places—even though the windbreaker was worn under a heavy

GI sweater. Yesterday—while I waited under a big leaning spruce—she came with fresh meat. She was no more than seven hundred feet away, and me with 6X field glasses—so I got a good show. She held the meat in one talon, and with the hooked beak, she tore off bite-sized pieces. Beak to beak, she gave it to the young who gathered in a half circle in front of her. Not once did they attempt to help themselves. They waited patiently for her to hand it to them. No sound, either. I wish you two could have been with me to watch that show! What she had killed, I couldn't tell, for I saw no feathers or skin.

Not long ago, I was filming a cow moose with twins—up by Hope Creek. I had been waiting there nearly eight hours. Finally, they left the brushy creek bottom to climb the bank—to a nice long grassy meadow with brush at both ends. There she started to romp with both twins. Finally, she chased them, and they ran as if their lives depended on it. With head down and ears back, she ran them into the brush—only to go out and wait for them to appear and streak for the other end. She would chase them again—and again. They made the run several times—as though they knew it was a must! Was it play—or a lesson? She was telling them what to do—it seemed. Once—when I was near—I saw small calves leave their mother and take off over a rise. A few minutes later, she followed—and so did I, but I didn't see them, nor her. Moose show uncommon intelligence. Some say God had a lot of parts left over from making the other animals, and tossed them together to make the moose—giving them lots of brains. (*of course, Doris and Flo say God knew precisely what He was doing and made just enough workable parts!* (smile!))

I'm wondering what you have for blueberries this time. Spring was late here, and it was several degrees warmer at blossom time. In some places it was just *pink* with blossoms. I saw blossoms where I had never seen them before. I watched for insect activity, but saw no unusual amount. Now the berries are small and not easy to see unless you examine closely. I'm afraid to look, for being disappointed. Some day they will be good sized berries or none at all. If rain makes for blueberries, there should be enough for the wild bunch *and me*.

Yesterday—on the creek flat near the hawk's nest—I saw a big rabbit. I hadn't seen one in years, and not even tracks of one in the past couple winters. This one was an Arctic Hare, and no doubt about it. It travels like a Jack Rabbit—not like the Cotton Tail and Snowshoe. Also, on the flat, I picked up a piece of jawbone with two teeth in place—molars of a meat-eater, and one of them very large, very old and worn. It must be from a big brown bear that lived many years ago. No doubt the bone washed down from up the creek somewhere. I had seen only one bear this year—a nice dark brown one, maybe a seven and a half or eight-footer.

Company from Port Alsworth had a New York family up here in a rubber raft—man, wife and daughter. They seemed to enjoy *"One Man's Wilderness."* It was beautiful weather for the most part. I had a couple from Fairbanks for ten days—he and I worked together on a ranch in Oregon back in the 1940's. He hasn't changed a bit—no hurry, and all the time in the world—stops paddling and waves his arms while singing a song. He has the perfect wife—just perfect for him. She doesn't attempt to change him; loves him for who he is. Just had a party of four here, Hank R.'s pilot and three from the Alaska Mountaineering Club. A party of eighteen camped at Postage Lake will be passing here on their way to Turquoise in a couple days. They wanted to know if they needed a raft to cross between these lakes. Crossing the Kijik could be much worse; in this weather, hiking is for the ducks. Florence, wish your picture-snapping brother Ed could have visited

Twin Lakes on a nice bright day. Green is at its very best now. Seems there is a bit more snow than in years past. Say! It just hit me—I can ferry that hiking-party across from one side of this water system to the other with my canoe—save them a wetting.

Still it rains a good blueberry-growing rain. Hope you two are enjoying a good summer season—happy as clams. My best, Dick

P.S. Hello and best wishes to Ruth and Pete.

Mama Goshawk

Watchful!

Twin Lakes
September 19, 1982

Dear Doris and Florence,

No lawn for me—just let it be. I wish you could see my front yard this morning. It is very red, yellow, green, brown and a mixture of all. The south slope across the lake is very yellow and this north slope, mostly red—beautiful fall colors.

Thank you for the real nice letter of August 9. It came in just before Glen flew me to the Bonanza Hills—Terry and Vic's camp. The closest he can land on floats is about one hour and twenty minutes from their camp. The landing place is two small lakes—connected by a narrows—at the head of Tom Creek. One time I was there when the Dolly Vardon were rising—so many, that the lake was alive with rises. I was with Terry and Vic from August 27 to September 5. Glen picked me up at the lakes again for the trip home.

Movies would be nice, but I'm afraid we would have to pull the plugs on all the TV's or we wouldn't have an audience. I'm not sure T.V. is for the best. It is a great thief of time, and money that often enough could be used for family necessities. I wrote to my brother, Raymond, in Lynwood, CA, and told him I was expecting the Park Service or Glen in soon. I would ask whoever came to call him and have him send up a couple of films from his collection. He could send them U.P.S. to Anchorage where Glen could pick them up before spud-digging time. Well, now it is spud-digging time and the letter I wrote is still here—and no plane has landed. So we *couldn't* have them by spud-digging time. Raymond has my 16mm movies and 35mm slides. I mail all of my films to him for processing and storage. I have seen very little of the film I have exposed. He runs it and reports on how I am doing. Maybe we can have him send some up—when the new wears off of TV. *(Yes, Dick—it doesn't seem to wear off for some. Maybe it is addictive—like drugs or a great bowl of popcorn?!)*

I found *Terry* and Vic looking good. It is too bad September 15th and time to leave was near. Vic was doing really well on her one and a half hikes to the diggings—and the half is a good climb. She will spend the winter at Bakers again and next spring she will have lost what weight she may have gained.

Going there from Tom Creek Lakes, I came over the brow of a hill to find a large, blonde grizzly directly ahead. It was busy digging for a parky squirrel and I didn't want to intrude—so took a detour under the curve of the hill to windward. No doubt the bear may have caught my scent, but didn't come to investigate.

A week-ago-today a real nice grizzly (brown bear) appeared here on my beach and not more than fifty feet from me—in front of the cabin. Not at all spooky, and I wish I had kept quiet and learned just how close it would come. Black bears are a nuisance and destructive. I order them to "git!" Not thinking, I did that with this beautiful, round-as-a-barrel, light and silky-coated brownie. It turned to go, went to the beach, and came right back as close as before— showing me how brave a bear can be with man-scent everywhere. It walked away and from the creek-flat I saw it traveling the lake shore headed down country. In all of my fourteen years in this cabin, that was the second brownie to come visit.

This morning, six rams—two good big ones— are on the slope of Bell Mountain, the mountain behind the cabin. They have circled the mountain as I do—and guided hikers at times. If you walk all the time, you two would enjoy my six-hour cir-cle-the-mountain tour.

29

I thought the mission girls would be in before now. Hollis T. told me, "I'll fly the mission girls in." Paul H. said the same. Sometimes I think Park Service goes south with the robins—I don't see them anymore.

Yes, I did get the permanent fund check and I didn't fill out a form this year. I did send one in last year, 1981. I'm sure you two can make good and worthwhile use of your check. Florence got her front tooth fixed, and Doris will buy a new set with hers. (*Not yet, Dick....!*) There is a saying, "Ignore your teeth and they will go away." My older sister, Helen, ended up with all of her natural teeth pulled. Now she is having a terrible time with dentures—gums aren't right and they don't fit or stay in place. Last I heard, she was having her gums built up by surgery. The surgeon says he can help her seventy-five percent towards better denture fit. Doris, I think you and I had better go see the dentist. My excuse is "I never lived where dentists grow." Have you heard of dental implants? They put artificial teeth in permanent by anchoring them to the jaw bone. I'm interested. Write for a free brochure *"A Patients Guide to Dental Implants"* 515 Washington St. PO Box 2002, Abington, MA 02351. (*Hey, Dick*—I do have dental stories, and one implant, but *please*, no set!)

I think electricity will be a great thing for you two—no more light-plant and all the mess that goes with it. You can do without the weight of those full fuel barrels.

Doris, your Mother has certainly done well, and I hope she continues to avoid surgery. At her age and condition, I would agree with the doctors that say "no!"

I wish you could see my new "Old Glory." I fly the flag every day, and mine was getting very faded and tattered. Assistant to the Secretary of Interior had said he would send a new one. In due time a box came, and in it a five by eight foot flag came—about twice the size of mine—and with it a very impressive-looking certificate. It stated the flag had been flown over the U.S. Capitol for me on July 29, 1982—by request of the honorable Ted Stevens, Senator of Alaska. So, come see my new flag.

"Mountaineering Club of Alaska" brought eighteen hikers—ten or eleven girls and women. They came from Portage Lake to be picked up here—and since then, many nice things have come my way: a beautiful rag-knit sweater, chocolates, sausages, banana-bread, etc.—and a promise to come again.

Closing for now—hoping all is well with you two. Thank you again for the good letter and the little book "*My Search.*" My Best, Dick.

Terry and Vicki Gill's Camp at Bonanza Hills

TWIN LAKES
OCTOBER 8, 1983

(Miner-Stamp-Picture stamped at top of page—
the same, plus a Moose-Stamp-Picture on envelope)
addressed to: Florence and Doris "The Mission Girls"

Dear Florence and Doris,

Thank you, Florence, for your good letter and
the September-October *Our Daily Bread*. It was
September 16th when you wrote. It was that afternoon when Leon and Joyce Hooley came to take
me out to harvest potatoes—a real nice day, and
Leon is a good little pilot. Perhaps he has his
Private license by now, and working towards his
Commercial. He will be flying for Glen before we
realize he is no longer the little boy who trudged to
school from the mission house.

Doris, I heard—and I'm truly sorry that it had
to be—your Mother was a very strong person to
carry on when the odds were so against her. God
bless her and you.

I'm sorry that it didn't work out that you could come to Twin Lakes with Babe. He could have fulfilled his promise to bring you, and you could have enjoyed a promise fulfilled. Good that you did get to see Cheryl's show and slides of Twin Lakes Country. As it stands now, I am to meet her and Fred in Anchorage before October 15th. Whether to drive the Highway or ride the ferry, we are not sure. It depends on weather and road conditions. After mid-October, a DC-10 is really the way to go—my opinion.

Karen did write after returning from *Gates of the Arctic*. How did she vote? Even-up, no contest, both perfect—like comparing mountain flowers with blueberries—so different, but both perfect. Evidently, she hit the weather just right there—as she did here: very few insects, the weather real nice, the hiking terrain good, few tussocks and hummocks. I'm glad it was a draw. She was nice.

I enjoyed Andy's stay at the lower end very much. Several times I heard his kicker and saw the big raft scooting up the lake. My mail had come to his cabin, so he brought it up. Of course, he had to stay for the following meal—and once he stayed overnight. Good business by the Park Service to hire the natives. John Branson was here a few days, and we hiked into Snipe Lake country—looking for an old native trap-line cache. Last day, Andy went with us to look for a cabin built by his grandfather—on the native trail from Lake Clark to Telaquana. We didn't find the cache that John and I searched for—good searchers but poor finders, I guess. Anyway, Andy invited us to have Indian Stew at his cabin. I had some cooked beans to add to the pot. Pretty good, and I asked him how he makes his Indian Stew. *"Oh, very easy, dice up some moose meat, boil it and stir in a little flour, a little salt if you have some, and pepper too."* Moose with white sauce, I call it. Good man, that Andy. Two or three times he told me of his life and how he quit alcohol *cold turkey*. He must be highly respected in Nondalton.

Say, you girls should go along on a Chilikadrotna River float sometime. I'm sure that you would enjoy it very much. Did I write that I floated it with Rangers, Maggie (5'2") and Clair R?

Little Maggie was ranger in *Gates of the Arctic* last year. It was a *clean-up* float in a five-man raft. Next time down, it will be clean—like a first-time floated river. Floaters are good people. We found very little that they left. Most was from hunting camps years back. We saw King Salmon every hour we were in the water, lots of bird-life—some I seldom see here—and lots and lots of blueberries.

Two days ago I called a bull moose to within one hundred feet of me. I knew there was the big bull and a cow in a huge brush patch, so at the edge and fifteen feet above the ground in a spruce tree, I imitated the grunting call of the moose. Unnn-nah! Near as I can describe it. I was surprised when the cow appeared out of a brushy draw, and then the big guy—ears forward they came—stopping often to look and listen. A second cow and smaller bull broke cover and followed. Slowly they came with me talking moose language. Finally, there I was up among the boughs with four moose—within rock-throwing distance.

That big guy was a nice one—a real nice rack, good spread, nice palms of a rich brown color, ten points on the right and eleven on the left. There was a fresh breeze coming down from Law Pass, and I was chilled good, but I hated to move them—so I toughed it out until they moved out of sight. One cow wasn't satisfied, and came to stand a hundred feet away. I had to go, so I climbed down. She stayed until I reached the ground, and then trotted away a few yards to stand and watch me leave. *What kind of moose is that*, she must have thought.

How did your potato crop turn out? We got a lot of potatoes—Laddy estimated 1800 to 2000 lbs. Lots of nice sized, but many smaller—good boiled with jackets on.

I smoothed both runways. Glen was busy flying hunters—and caribou hunting, himself. Leon went hunting, too. I had it planned that I would say, "Let's go visit the Mission Girls" when there came a break in their busy schedule. Then, Glen, Pat, Leon and Daniel went to Anchorage for a couple days, and also, the wind blew fierce. I was scheduled to come back by way of Hollis and the Park Service 185 as soon as the wind calmed a bit. While waiting, I worked around the ranch—cleaning up, picking rocks and working on the three-wheeler, *Big Red*. The trip to Twin Lakes was delayed from one day to the next. Finally, we would give it a try. "*Nothing to stop us but fear and common sense*," Hollis said. So we came, and it was a nice trip. Wish I could have made it to Nondalton. Maybe I can, before I go back to Twin Lakes—after going Outside. Both of you will be there then. I think Doris must have been away while I was out for potato harvest. Some day we will get together for a good visit—and a big bowl of popcorn. Did you pop some while Babe and Mary were there? Doesn't Babe look to be in perfect health? He may out-live us yet. Maybe we should move to the Big Island, too.

Wishing you girls good health and just lots and lots of happiness—never saw you otherwise. Have a real good winter season. Best of wishes, Dick

Yes, Andy deserved a lot of respect

Picnic from the pack

TWIN LAKES
DECEMBER 21, 1983

Dear Doris and Florence,

Thank you for the good letter, the pictures, "*Our Daily Bread*" and the calendar. Only two calendars until now, and I don't expect more.

I arrived in Anchorage on December 15th and came to Port Alsworth with Mark Lang that same day. I wish you could have seen that loaded 185 plane. Mark's wife, Sandy, Dave's wife, Jacque—and Lang's little Dustin in the rear seat—sacks and boxes under, over and on all sides—Really packed in, but not a heavy load. Mark is a good pilot and keeps the conversation going.

Moose Hunting was the rage at the farm. I'm doubtful that I had safe ice to land here anyway. Hollis reported my lake being iced over no more than four or five days. It's very mild, so I might have to stay at Lake Clark—unless I wanted to walk seven and a half miles up from the extreme lower end—whenever the Bay gains ten miles of ice.

December is ending on the mild side—three degrees below, until now. Isn't this nice winter weather? Have a nice day—plane day tomorrow, perhaps.

There were no moose for Glen, Dave or Leon and they came home early. Leon—with his brand-new private pilot's license would fly me in. Daniel would ride the baggage compartment, and they would look for moose on the way home. Two heavy rocks came in with us—December 17th. Dropped one, and it went through the ice. The second one opened a hole, but lay a few feet away. Young and bold Leon said, "I think it's safe enough." I said, "No, let's go to the lower end." Leon said, "Let's try it." So, we made a touch and go—no stop, for then is a critical time. We went around and came in again—stopped and no cracking. He chopped a hole in the ice to find it four inches strong. Good enough. Leon had saved me a lot of miles on foot.

There was a foot of snow and many, but old, moose tracks. There was an imprint on the beach where a moose had bedded down. One of my robber-birds came while I shoveled snow. It came to my hand as if I hadn't been away. Until now, I haven't seen sheep. The wind is strong on the mountain, and they would seek shelter in a canyon or on the lee-side of the mountain. I see no rabbits, but their population is at extreme low cycle at this time of year. Today I have four birds, the same number I had before leaving. So, I'm settled in and ready for Christmas and the New Year.

I do hope that you two have a good holiday season. I have heard in the past, "The Mission Girls are afraid to fly." I didn't think so, judging from all the times they have flown and seemed to enjoy it— even Doris when Grandpa Babe insisted she fly the T-Craft to Port Alsworth.

(Grandpa Babe's idea, not ours! It was his way of giving us a flying lesson! Taking Flo and Doris one at a time—he in the passenger seat! After all, he could fly from either seat, equally as well! But the east wind was blowing, and we were bouncing around! Upon landing at Port A, Babe says, "Well, you can fly alright, but you'd probably kill yourself on landing." Was that a grin?)

Thanks for letting me see the pictures. Your nephew Randy is a worker. The cabin, though like mine, has a lower door. He used many logs and small ones. The cabin is high, so it must have a loft. I would like to meet him sometime. You say the cabin is up north? Do you know where exactly— as far north as the Arctic Circle? *(No, Montana!!)*

While here, Babe wanted to buy film to show in Hawaii. I had none that I thought satisfactory, so had my brother in Arlington, VA to get a copy of *"One Man's Wilderness"* for Babe and Mary. I hope they enjoy it and treat friends and neighbors to a show. Remember the film I ran at Nondalton years back? Do you think it would be of interest in Nondalton again? It is the best show I have, I think, and I brought it along. I plan to let the Park Service show it—and possibly have it copied if they are interested. Hollis seems very much interested and said, "I'll fly you out, and we will have a show." Perhaps we can show it at Nondalton, too, if you think it interesting after so many years. (*In time, the film was shown on several T.V. Stations.*)

Thanksgiving? Yes, we did have a good day. My Sis, Helen, asked me what I would like for dinner. Helen is one to go all-out and was surprised when I said, "A large bowl of hot Chili!"

I figured that would save her a lot of work— which it did—but no turkey.

Hope you two have had a real nice *fall season* until now, and that you did have a real nice *holiday season*. My Best Always, Dick.

Jasper, Jenny, and Junior

Feeding the triplets

44

Twin Lakes
March 9, 1984

Dear Doris and Florence,

It is 3:30 A.M. now, and the sun is trying to break through. It rained a little this morning, the first rain of '84. Then a breeze came up the lake and it snowed *goose-feather frost* for a while. It has been mild springtime since March 1st. There has only been a three-degree spread in temperature these past four days. That is two readings per day, so it held constant—the reason being a strong southeast wind from the gulf.

Thank you for your good letter, Florence. Clair told me about the gang staying at the mission during the tournament. Port Alsworth has quite a school now, and is fortunate to have Daniel with his basketball experience.

How did the boys get that chimney fire going? I remember the local country store back home with its huge pot-bellied stove and long, long stove pipe. It needed cleaning out, and one of the local loafers knew just how to do it. Walt Pool was his name. He filled an empty fruit can with kerosene, tossed it and closed the door. Whoosh! It wasn't long until the stove pipe was red—up to the brick chimney. They thought Walt had over-done for a little while.

It was good of those guys to work up your wood and stack it. With five working, a lot *could* be accomplished if the wood lengths were *near*—or if standing timber was *available*.

Here, winter didn't get started until I came back from Miller Creek. I had gone down to help John cut and skid in cabin logs. The good grove of log-trees he had his eye on turned out to be on native allotment land—unavailable. So we had to march up Miller Creek, beyond Jay and Bella's property line. We only found about thirty, and those were not all usable for logs. John called it off, and gave what we had cut to Jay. Jay had a couple small jobs for me, too. After four to five days, Bee came for me and flew me home.

Starting January 21st, winter set in for a week— with minus 41 degrees the low. Then came February, and winter from the start. Morning average temperature for the first fifteen days was minus 15.46— the last fourteen days minus 3.5—only four days of February with both morning and evening readings above zero. Broke a record this time—a minus 56 after being minus 25 and an up-lake wind in the afternoon. Slow in warming: a minus fifty at ten, and minus forty-eight at noon. I hoped for a minus sixty next night, and it was plus 20 degrees with a southeast wind.

There have been lots of beautiful, bright, calm days—with good deep snow-cover, undisturbed by wind. I thought of you two and wished you could see Twin Lakes today. The snow-pack was thirty-two inches at best, and the lake ice now twenty-seven inches. Sure looks like an early breakup. It was thirty-three and one-half last year, and gone May 26th.

Sheep seem to have winterized good, and my best count was fifty-plus, but not more than fifty-five—with several real nice rams in the bunch.

For eight days now, I have had a cow moose and coming-yearling-bull calf nearby with antler stubs about one and one-half inches. The moose seem very tame. Just yesterday, the cow came as close as eight feet from me to pick dead willow leaves. I could easily reach out and touch her nose with my five-foot walking staff. I've seen no rabbits, so small meat-eaters are very scarce here. Regarding the film, when there is no longer danger of freezing in my cabin, we will try to arrange a show at Port Alsworth and Nondalton, OK? Glen said last time in, "Maybe Dad can fly the mission girls in while he is here this time." They would like to get Babe's brother Lloyd to Port Alsworth at the same time. (*Flo and I remember meeting Lloyd—perhaps in Spokane, WA. He looked a lot like Babe, but was taller.*)

Well, must close for now. Hope this finds you two your usual cheerful selves. Have a real nice spring season. My Best, Dick.

Twin Lakes
July 4, 1984

Dear Doris and Florence,

What a pretty day for the 4th of July—cotton clouds, a fair breeze up the lake and fifty-six degrees. (I like my temperatures much better than yours.) I have my five by eight foot flown-over-the-U.S. Capitol flag flying this special day. I fly the three by five duralite—all other days—which, though smaller, has a bright, slick finish and is very durable.

A few days ago, two plane loads of visitors came from a lodge at Port Alsworth. *Some guy had the nerve to ask me if the mission girls in the book are real or just fiction. Why the nerve of some people's kids!!* I guess you know I squared him away on that. Thank you for your good letter of way back, March 23[rd.] You're thinking about going out pretty quick then—and someone recently said you would be back in July—I figured it would be the first half of July if you wanted to get some garden in.

Doris, I hope you had no more trouble with the fish poison. I have never had it. Is it common? I still have some of that good fish you sent up—saving some for an Iowa-farmer neighbor and his Californian executive brother—due here July 26th for one week. I have requested they bring catsup so we can *catch-up* on everything. Did you know I was at Port Alsworth in early April to work on Glen's D-4 Cat? He flew me out the 6th for about a week. I took the film along in case it worked out that we could get to Nondalton. I mentioned it, but it didn't work out. With you kids leaving—or already gone—it wouldn't have been the best time. Fred Hirschmann of the Park Service is the entertainer. I offered the use of the film for the season, but I haven't seen them for quite some time. I was told they are presently pretty busy on the coast of the Inlet. If they do use it, I would like to be present for the first show—to acquaint Fred with the film and narration. Fred would do a good job. We had a show in the new school at Port Alsworth, but not under ideal conditions. The screen is high—on the wall of the gym—and there is no way to darken that row of high windows. Therefore, we had the show in a small, too warm room with no windows—projecting onto a bare wall that was not the best.

It was good to hear of Pete and Ruth. How long has it been since I saw you two and them? They should be pretty well up in years it seems. I don't know about you and Six Mile Lake, but here at Twin Lakes time spent is a *bonus* and not counted in your life span—*says so in the Book*. It must be mostly true, since I see no extra effort required to climb the mountains since the Book came out. I do find it a bit easier to sleep later after a tough day. *(Psalm 90:10; Psalm 91:14-16 Answer)*

It has been a good year here at the Lakes. Ice went out of the lake on June 4th, with only twenty-six inches—the least ever to go. First new lambs showed on May 10. There were no more until May 15—then lambs most every day.

I saw the first bear on April 19th—on the shore of the lower lake—and saw four more after that. One was not just an ordinary bear. (Excuse please—had to get my sourdough biscuits in the oven.) This bear was maybe a seven-foot brownie—everyone likes to call them grizzlies, which sounds fierce. I saw this one chasing a young cow moose. It lost her, and hit *my* track. Here it came with the wind in its favor; me with only my walking staff and one runty spruce about twelve feet tall. That bruin kept coming—nose to the ground—and I kept thinking he would quit

51

my track and leave. Wrong! It got too late for me to leave, so I climbed the little tree and took my staff along so I could punch him in the nose if he was determined to scratch my feet. He stopped at about twenty-five feet and looked for me. Surprise is half the battle, they say, so I yelled real loud and shook that tree-top fiercely! The poor guy nearly sat down before he turned and walked the other way—only to turn and take a few steps back—then turn again and amble slowly away. I watched until he was out of sight in the brush, then I climbed down and came home to see what my robbers were doing.

Two days later, I was heading down the ice to see if I might see him or his tracks. Who did I see, but Mr. Bear, coming up the shore-line. I waited here at the cabin feeling I was on his visitors' list. I heard a noise in the brush behind the cabin. I climbed to the cabin roof to see, and there he was—about fifty yards back—wrangling with an old dry moose hide. Mr. Bear had pulled it down from a spruce where I had hung it. He was biting and bending, popping and cracking it. He was on his feet, on his back—it seemed he was playing with it—looked at me and then back to his plaything until he tired of it. He went on to the woodshed, but he didn't enter. He turned and went on his way. Giving him a good lead, I followed, and saw him traveling the ice along shore—heading for the upper end. I may know that bear. A brownie his color had come to my beach and out front. Thinking of the black-bear, a nuisance when they want to be, I hollered, "You had better get going." He went, but took his time. A tame-acting bear was seen a couple of times at the stream between the lakes. It must have been the same bear. Just two days ago—up Hope Creek—I saw a mother bear with a small cub—the first cub in a couple of years.

Nine Sierra Club hikers, including seven girls, passed here—heading from Turquoise Lake to Lake Clark. They travel coast to coast—and Florida. It was nice to hear them on a timber trail—lots of whooping, bells jingling, hands clapping etc. I told them they would never see a bear—with that much *racket*. (June is moose-calf hunting time for the bears.)

I went to the sheep-lick June 26th finding about seventy head there. I had company from Florida for six days—and couldn't go sooner. I suspect I was too late to see them all.

Judging from blossoms, I predict a very skimpy blueberry crop—sorry about that.

For supper this evening: half of an eighteen-inch lake-trout, sourdough biscuits, red radishes and dessert—cold porridge pudding and a cup of hot lemonade. That's all there is—wishing you two a real good rest of summer. Dick. P.S. Hope you both had a real nice vacation *outside*. Wish you could come and stay a few days some nice weather spell. I would turn my cabin over to you.

Ruth and Pete

Twin Lakes
October 13, 1984

Dear Doris and Florence,

It looks just like winter here today: foggy, fast-moving clouds, rough lake, noisy surf on my beach and ten inches of snow. The temperature isn't so winterish at twenty-seven degrees.

I have been writing letters today—sorting and burning old ones. I'm going south in April sometime, and will be gone for a couple months. Never did hear that you came back, but feel certain that you did. Today, too, I ran across a clipping on fish poisoning and thought of you, Doris. Perhaps you will find it interesting. No answer to my last letter to the Mission girls. I remember telling you I had been in Port Alsworth to help Glen work on his poor, miserable, broken-down D-4 Cat. Well, I have been there three times since September 10th. Helped harvest potatoes, a real nice crop of maybe six thousand pounds. Glen used *Conklin* liquid fertilizer, and I'm convinced that it was worth it.

Nicest potatoes I have helped harvest there in a long time. There was a small crew this time. For hours at a time, I was just *lonesome me* in the patch. Sure did miss Terry and Vic. They went to Anchorage just a few days before. Everyone was busy, and the spuds got to the bin, so was it necessary to have a dozen people in the patch? Not necessary, *but less lonesome me!?*

Later, I was in for two and a half days to operate Bee's D-6 dozer—finding Mark's property end place, and again for the Park Service to landscape with the D-6 around the hanger they had leased from Bee. There is only one day and a half to complete that project. I stayed overnight at B's old house where the Park Service Ranger and Program Director lives. In the spring I had told him I wanted my film "The Frozen North" shown at Nondalton during his schedule for this year. I also requested that he announce the show be dedicated to "The Mission Girls". He told me this late September that he hadn't put on a show at Nondalton, but this October after the busy hunting season—patrol work in late August and September—he hoped to put on shows at Nondalton, Pedro Bay and other village sites. I do hope he gets that done. Seems we have been a long time with no show for you folk.

Guess you heard that Ranger Andy shot a bear on the Kijik that seemed determined to get to him and little Maggie—thought they were twin moose calves, I guess. For Andy, twenty feet was close enough. Then I had people from Texas and New York, and hikers from Palmer and Norway. A big double party—two groups of ten—stayed one week each. The leader and staff of four stayed two weeks. Though most of the people were from the Pacific Coast, one woman was from Madrid, Spain—a first for Twin Lakes. I have the Parklands book and the autograph of Bill Brown. I didn't know he was related to Andy. Guess you noticed my cabin, new and bright (page 59 I think.) The leader, author, lecturer and tour guide, was from Belleview, WA. The book "One Man's Wilderness" was the reason for their coming, he said. It was required reading for all who came. One day for each group was spent hiking to my cabin where their cook, a woman, put together a big lunch on the beach. My guest book collected a lot of names and much flattery. You must come add your names and read my guest book someday. I think it would be a best seller.

Two from Norway were the last—just camping, hiking and fishing a little. They enjoyed seeing the animals and watching a flickering camp fire. Just before they left, they spent part of the day here. We saw 25 sheep, two of which were rams and one a good one, two bull caribou and one a white-cape trophy bull. That made their day! I had canoed them across the rough lake, and although I thought it would be nothing for those North Sea natives, they thought it pretty rough. Maybe it was the canoe that made it seem so.

This spring was a good lambing—twenty-five to twenty-six—and the first lamb to die on the mountain. A broken neck, I learned and believe—a golden eagle chased it over a high rock face. Again, I visited the mineral lick in June and counted more than 70 sheep there.

I was below the lower lake when the caribou herd—cows, calves and a few bulls were there—thousands of them and I shot some movies. Six big rams summered on the mountain behind my cabin. I saw them often, and shot both 35mm (still) and 16mm movies.

One fine moose bull was the boss during moose-rut in early October. Filmed him one day, and the next I looked for him in the brush and heavy timber. Suddenly, there was loud grunting in the brush near-by, and here he came—slowly—and raking that big rack in the brush. I was behind a big dead snag with lots of low boughs. He came to within fifteen feet, his head down, breathing heavy and daring me to come out and fight. Guess you know, I was still as a mouse and trying to look that small. Would you believe that he spooked and turned to leave when I moved a bit to better concealment? Why, the big scaredy-cat—he lost a few points for bravery there.

Just a few days ago, I came into a small grizzly—with this year's twin cubs—digging wild pea vines. She was very lame in her left front leg or foot. I would have been happy to help her if it was agreeable. How can she dig a den for three? It would be like splitting spruce chunks with one hand. I must have watched them for thirty minutes—at 100 yards—before she got my scent and ran. And then it turned cooler, and it snowed again and again until now—ten inches. It's time for the bears to turn in. I'm not sure when plane day will be, but I hope for one more day before float season ends.

In closing I would like to say, hope you two had a real enjoyable and satisfying summer, and that winter will be both cold and mild to suit the taste of each. Please write and better still, come visit. Ok? Ok! Sincerely, Dick.

P. S. Almost forgot. I had a honeymoon couple from Pensacola, FL live in my cabin for a week in June; then two home-country brothers spent a week fishing in late July and August.

Now I have a wolf story for you. About a week ago I discovered many wolf tracks across the creek — tracks of a moose running, too. During my days search to solve the problem, I learned there were six wolves that had run the cow a mile before reaching here. Here, they gave up the chase — and was it because I was here? If so, I'm glad, for according to the tracks, that moose was scared! As the wolves retreated down country, I found six beds where they had curled to sleep. In deep snow they traveled single file, with followers using the leader's tracks. I would have liked to see them doing that.

No plane to land since October 18th, but an air-drop of mail by Hollis November 20th when your letter came. Now for freeze-up and landing ice by Christmas. I have a bundle of Christmas letters to go, but if they don't mail by next week, next month they will. If you are rushed doing your letters, I can wait. I am a patient one. Wishing you — and everyone every-where — all the best. Sincerely, Dick Proenneke.

A shovel full of snow

TWIN LAKES
DECEMBER 6, 1984

Dear Doris and Florence,

Merry Christmas to you, too! It's a small chance that you will read this before that special day. No ice until now—the lake as blue and lively as in summer time. Thank you for your welcomed letter and *Our Daily Bread*. Now if only I had Babe here to read it his own special way. Babe is a real good reader—guess you know.

Sure was good to hear from you two—and that everything is fine with you. I'm wondering if you will get to Port Alsworth by Christmas. You could go by boat, no doubt. Surely you don't have ice in Six Mile Lake already, or is it quick and easy to ice over? My lower lake closed up on November 9th, and now has eleven inches of ice. This one is cold enough, but the wind blows and blows. Today is the first day with an up-lake wind—sign of cold—in a long time. Winds from the gulf—south east—are always warm. Just a day or two ago, it was 37 degrees, and there were many days above 30 degrees. There were only ten inches of snow from November 1st until now, and in the woods, ten inches is the snow-pack. Doris, are you the poet? Arctic Echoes reads real nice. Good to see you two again, if only on the front page. Someday you two will make the book come true by walking up the path to my cabin. I want you to know I have a good supply of popcorn on hand, and if I am too excited to remember, remind me.

I had two men from home for a week of fishing. Brothers—one a farmer and the other a Senior Vice President of *Hunt Food*—so we had a big jug of good catsup and 15 pounds of popcorn. In case you haven't heard, Hunt Foods bought out Orville Redenbacher and his world's best popcorn. They still use his name, because he is the best-looking guy in town.

You have been busy, and I can imagine you came home to find the garden was hiding in the weeds. I'll bet Glen sure had a nice crop at Port Alsworth, and I could have used a couple good picker-uppers. The faithful's, Terry and Vic, left for Anchorage before harvest. Seems everyone had their own project going—not like the good old Babe and Mary days when we had ten or a dozen in the patch. For hours at a time, I was the plower-outer and picker-upper— Laddy busy at the root-cellar sorting and storing.

Really nice potatoes—medium, large and smooth. Glen applied some good Conklin fertilizer, and I do believe it was responsible. It was liquid, and I wish you girls could try it in your little 4X4 patch up by your house. *(Grandpa Babe always used chicken happiness from the chicken house—mixed with dirt from the goat barn.)* On our big patch by the lake, we used commercial fertilizer, 8-32-16. Around the rhubarb we stacked chicken happiness from Babe and Mary's, and the rhubarb thrived!!

I sure do hope Ranger Fred got to Nondalton with my film before his season ended. I requested he dedicate the show to the Mission Girls. He would do that.

Filming? I did a pretty good job on Caribou, Moose and Sheep this summer. There were thousands of caribou below the lower lake. The best bull moose in the woods, and his following in mid-October. Did I write about him hearing me and coming through heavy timber and brush—slowly raking that huge rack in the brush—talking low with that course, grunting cough? Makes one's heart beat faster when he just keeps coming! Big Dall rams, six of them, just above tree line behind my cabin—across the creek and on the lower slope of Cow gill Mountain

Twin Lakes
February 27, 1985

Dear Florence and Doris,

Greetings from the frozen North. It has been a snowy day with falling temperature. Plane day is coming soon. I'm writing a batch to go, and your good, short letter of December 26 came to the top of my priority stack. I'll write a short one before it comes time to go check the snowfall for the last 24 hours. Maybe one-third of a mile from here is a big log across a ditch. It is located in an open spot in heavy timber. The snow never drifts there, and I can get an accurate check. I clean the test area after each check. As of yesterday, the total for the snow season is real close to 132 inches, with snow-pack (total accumulation settled) about 38 inches. In some places snow is packed so solid it will carry a moose. I was glad to get your little letter. Glen told me the sad news concerning Tony.

Regarding the B.I.A. houses, are there many? What type of construction—are they frame or pre-fab? Ruth and Pete built a new log cabin as I remember. Say, how do you like my new stamp? How has your winter been? Here, January had a morning average temperature of 28.06 degrees for the month. That's tropical. December was the snow month with fifty-five inches. February was the winter one with eighteen days, averaging 29.97 degrees, and ten days of that was minus 30 to minus 44 degrees, clear and calm—beautiful weather. I wish you could have enjoyed my snow scenery— no snow-machine tracks—no ski tracks—just the tracks of my snowshoes and the wild ones.

Two sheep died that I am aware of. One, a fine full-curl ram, was smothered by an avalanche. After I helped the ravens dig it out, it became food for ravens, magpies, lynx cat, my robber birds and the red fox. Because of some meat here, a martin came. At last, I saw one after seeing tracks for several winters—tracks that I felt certain were martin. Have you girls ever seen one running free? Please ask Pete and Ruth if they have. Ask if the martin were light or dark in color. This one was very light with a whitish throat and I am wondering if the orange-throated martin are naturally darker in color. I saw this one by flash-light, and for maybe a couple minutes as it nosed around looking for scraps.

I hear that Lake Clark finally iced over, and a pack of ten wolves were seen at the outlet—or near it. This lake closed up December 14th, and now it has only 18 inches of ice—due to an early break-up, I'd say, for it has good packed snow-cover. Moose are using it in their travels up and down. Nearly a dozen went up a few nights ago, and two cows headed down—stopped here for a day. They appeared to be in good condition, but it is a long time until June and new willow feed.

Did I tell you that St. Nick came to Twin Lakes by helicopter on December 23rd? It was a very stormy day, and certainly no one should be flying, but I heard an airplane engine. Here came Bee and Glen out of the white. Who says there isn't a Santa Clause! "No problem," says Glen. I think those kids (Bee and Glen) are the birds next of kin—but doing them one better, for the birds didn't fly that day.

Closing for now, and thinking of you two. Please continue your good health. Have a real nice rest of winter, OK? Truly, Dick.

TWIN LAKES
APRIL 12, 1985

Dear Florence and Doris,

Just a few lines to say thanks for coming; thanks for all the goodies—really, you shouldn't have; thanks for the good visit—thanks for everything. It was just the greatest thing that has happened to Twin Lakes, and I wish all the readers of the book (One Man's Wilderness) knew that you finally made it. I have received lots of letters asking if the Mission Girls ever made it to Twin Lakes.

If I had known or even suspected you were coming, I would have had my diggings looking much better. Normal spring I would have had my house cleaning done and heavy winter clothes put away, but April is still mid-winter. Yesterday morning minus 34 degrees, and this morning minus 24 degrees—to make the morning average temperature for April a minus 14 degrees.

You flew away, and I hope you had an enjoyable flight back to Nondalton. How old was Leon when

Babe first said "I am going to fly the Mission Girls in to see Twin Lakes"? (He may still have been in the cornered pants.) The day after you left here, I climbed the mountain to sheep country. It was very cold up there, and usually it is much warmer than on the lake. Still, there were twenty-nine sheep acting content with their diet of snow—and little else. I wish it would warm and give them a break.

Yesterday, I thought of you two and your skimpy wood situation—while I cut a good dead tree and sledded in four good loads. Wood was scarce near Nondalton before the private land. Now it must be near impossible.

It is over-cast and minus 24 degrees this morning. Now at 11:30, it is plus 5 degrees and clear. I'm expecting Leon with my tape material at any time. I should have asked him to come the 14th or 15th. Now I feel I must stay close every day until he comes.

In storing all the goodies that came with you, I thought, "Who am I to deserve such kindness? Your cake, pie, little turkey, cookies and all the rest. I know you won't take payment for it, but would you please cash the enclosed check and use the money as you see fit? Buy some wood—or for provisions to make more cakes, pies and cookies for your visitors to the Mission, OK? I would be pleased if you did. Just don't know who to make this check out to, so "heads to Florence—tails to Doris." Heads it was. Best to you both, Dick

Swede saws hanging. Maul in hand.

Twin Lakes
April 14, 1985

Dear Florence and Doris,

This morning, the wind came South-Southeast, and winter ended with a 17 degree reading. Now at 10:15 a.m. the wind is very strong down, the temperature 30 degrees.

Do you know, those cookies would soon be gone if I kept them in the cabin—not keeping worth a cent, so I moved them to the cache. Want a cookie? Climb the ladder. I am enjoying that real good whole wheat bread. I can't remember when I have tasted better—or as good. It is very light for whole wheat. John Branson used to make whole wheat, but don't go near the lake if you eat it. *The inference meaning you would sink??—Mary Alsworth taught the Mission Girls, and probably John, too* 😊.

This morning, I made an all-out-search and found the makings for a new dish washer—and made one. Foam rubber and nylon mesh is the material. A couple years ago, an Oregon fisherman gave me the nylon, saying it was good for making a dish washer. I put it away so well that I couldn't find it when my present one expired. (Doris, I wouldn't have let you see that miserable thing and should have hidden it.)

Now what if it turns warm? My birthday treats—the little turkey and the banana cake—would not keep three weeks. The pieces of pie became smaller and smaller—until yesterday evening saw the last of it.

"Tell you what I'm gonna do!" I have a good supply of those good square gas cans, and brand new. They have been in Hope's cabin since the early sixties. I'll make you a couple new pans and a good Dick Proenneke special dust or chip pan. Real good for managing chips from your woodpile—or for any use requiring a good, sturdy, sharp-edged pan to sweep into.

My robbers miss all the good company. They come, and if I am busy I ignore the racket out front. They soon leave and go to work for a living. I wonder how far they do range out. I have seen them across the creek and above the mountain timberline. A nest is what I would like to find—and have looked for several times in the spring. They are very secretive about their nest, and few people have seen one. You might ask Pete and Ruth if they have ever seen one. Some people are superstitious about the camp robber. According to some books, ill may befall them if they even look into the nest and count the eggs. R. L. P.

Twin Lakes
April 17, 1985

Waiting for the plane. The wind was strong the past two days, but this morning found it calm and 20 degrees. It snowed about one inch yesterday morning. April 15th was a nice day—with a high of 43 degrees. I cleaned house, and it now looks more presentable. I also took steel wool to my poor, old, miserable teakettle, and it sparkles. On the 14th I did make two gas can pans and a dust pan. Because Pete and Ruth were so kind and sent in the very good smoked salmon, I wish you would offer to give them one of the pans. They might enjoy one just for the novelty of the thing. The pans last much better after washing if you turn them bottom side up on the stove to dry. I suspect you used yours more as a garden pan when gathering vegetables. I hope you liked the dust pan—just right for scooping chips into your heater, or as a cleaning container when removing ashes.

Now, at 8 a.m. it is breezing up again. Have a nice day. R.L.P. P. S. If you have use for two pans, please let me know, for I have scads of cans, ok?

"Half a Gas Can"

Not understanding the language, our 2nd grade student pronounced Athabascan, "halfagascan". I do hope he and our friends are still able to smile with me on that one.

TWIN LAKES
APRIL 18, 1985

This evening, I will hike down to the stream between the lakes to see if the brave mallard pair have arrived. May see a bear track this time. I'm not sure how often someone visits Nondalton from Port Alsworth, so I have boxed and addressed the tin ware. I'm sure you will get it sooner by U.S. Mail. It was three degrees this early morning at 10 a.m. It is now 10 degrees, clear and calm. I'm waiting for the plane and writing letters while a pot of beans bubble — nearly ready to sample. I'm reminded of little Leon and Sig years back. I was working in the wood shed, and could hear the lid on the cooking beans rattling often — sampling, no doubt. R.L.P. P.S. Nice to have my fireplace uncovered. Wish you could see it. You two must come in again — in summer, blueberry time or fall colors.

Twin Lakes
June 7, 1985

Dear Doris and Florence,

It's a calm, damp, quiet 35-degree morning here. Light rain dimples the border of open water between lake ice and beach. The lake level is up 14 inches from winter low water—the snow nearly gone in my cabin area. I covered a three-foot-deep patch of it with many thicknesses of Visqueen and use it as cold storage for my egg supply. The temperature is close to 32 degrees. I still have miles of lake ice, but it is dark blue, and some good winds would see it gone in a few days. I feel sure it will be gone by June 16th and plane day.

Thank you for your nice letter of May 19th. I consider it number one of the all-time nice letters I have received. It is payment in full for any small favors on my part. If you were here this morning, we would dress for the *wet as sap* brush and go visit Susie the moose and her new single calf. Have you seen a very small moose calf? Reddish-brown and just as neat and trim as a merry-go-round fancy. It was born about four days ago, and not more than a ten-minute walk from here—in heavy brush, and I do well to see it. I go a couple times each day to see if I can convince old mom that I mean no harm. Until now, she isn't convinced, and if I get closer than fifty yards, she will come walking slowly towards me—acting as gentle as a milk cow—but I have seen that act performed a few times. Suddenly, she goes from gentle to violent—ears go flat back, and here she comes with those big teeth showing. She ends the charge by rearing and striking with those front feet. It is very frightening when you are in heavy brush and no chance to dodge. After she strikes, she will go back to her calf and may lay down—acting very unconcerned. So knowing all this, I start walking away when she keeps coming. This morning, her ears were just starting to go back, and she followed me farther than usual. She is located beyond Spike's cabin on the point, and I think it doubtful that a bear will find her there. They seem to follow the trails a lot in their search for calves, and she is not near a trail passing by. She was here on my beach a day or two before she calved, and knowing she was in the area, I searched until I found her.

Please excuse me if I repeat. I write many letters, and don't always remember where I was last
time. About May 15th many, many caribou came to
both sides of the lower lake. Hundreds of caribou
crossing the ice, and many bedded down on the
ice. The ice seems a favorite place for them to lie.
Calving time, but I saw no new calves. May 17th
I was there and saw a dark grizzly working both
sides of the lake—looking for calves. I doubt that
he found any, for I didn't see one with the hundreds
of caribou that moved out of his way onto the lake
ice—then they left the lower lake. On May 24th,
Hollis and I flew—looking for new calves. We saw
quite a sprinkling of them over towards the Stoney
River. May 10th showed the first new lamb on the
mountain, then no more for a few days. It was the
same last year, so one ewe must be the early bird.
By now, I think maybe fifteen lambs from a bunch
of about thirty-five sheep.

Say, I must not forget to mention May 4th, my
day. I saved one layer of the banana cake. For a
while, I thought I might have to order more cake
to make the frosting come out even. The frosting I
kept fresh by skimming the surface each day. Good
frosting. I buttered each slice of cake as I ate it. I
fried the little turkey golden brown and enjoyed it

for several days. The cookies—I still have a few in the cookie can up in the cache.

Of course, you didn't know, nor did I, that a big, dark-blond mama bear was in hibernation across the lake and down a half mile—when you were here. It was May 15th that I found her. Yes, she had cubs—cute twins, dark with white collars. One was a first of its kind. The white was behind the front legs as well as the front—as if the little guy poked his front legs down through the white. There was only a narrow white line behind the legs. Cubs are nothing but lively at their age. Twins have more fun than singles, I'm sure of it. On steep snow patches, they behave like Leon and Sig—when little—and mom joins in the fun, too, by running and sliding. One cub fight, and their little dog-fight voices could be heard on the lake as they tumbled down the mountain—tied in a hard knot. Old mom just stood and admired her little darlings. I saw them nearly every day until the last of May. I saw her try for a lamb, but its mom was just too smart for her. She saw the bear when it was coming down a steep rock face no more than thirty feet away. The lamb was laying close to the base of the wall. The ewe got the lamb out of sight around a rocky point—but refused to leave the protection of the steep face until the bear left. Then she took her lamb and left the area. So for two weeks, ewes, lambs and bears shared the same mountain side. The ewes with lambs were ever on the alert and gave the bear lots of room. On May 16th I located the hibernation den, and must climb to examine it after the ice goes out so I can canoe across.

Another first for Twin Lakes happened just a few days ago. Never had I found the nest of a spruce grouse (known as *fool hen*). This one not even one step from the trail, and she flushed when I passed, or I would never have found it. It was in the moss under low boughs of a runty little spruce tree. There were four eggs, cinnamon in color with dark brown spots and blotches. Every day I check, the number has increased. There were six yesterday. She was glued on tight, and maybe starting to incubate. Their usual number is ten to twelve—or maybe fourteen.

So, *One Man's Wilderness* has been especially good to me this spring, and to think you started it all with your visit that minus-twenty-degree clear, calm day. Don't forget blueberry time and the picnic on the mountain.

I'm glad the tin-ware was a hit. Which pan did you keep? One can had started to rust and may not last a long time. Would Ruth like a dust pan? I would be glad to make her one. If you can think of anything in the line of tin-ware that you can make use of, please mention it. I think I can make a pan in about twenty-five to thirty minutes. A dust pan takes less time. If we had lots of bright shiny gas cans, we could start a dust-pan factory to go along with the doll factory. I would like to see a real neat pan and dust-pan gold plated. At an auction in Anchorage I think they would go pretty high—just because they were made from the lowly gas can. Agree?

Still it is—dead calm, quiet and the cloud deck low. Light sprinkles still dimple the open water now at ten a.m. Closing for now, and wishing you girls—Ruth and Pete and everyone a real enjoyable late spring, early summer season. Best to you always, Dick.

P.S. I wonder, would you mind if the world learned that you finally made it to Twin Lakes? Just a lot of people would enjoy your visit if only to read that you were here.

June 9—that little grouse hen is the greatest. Glued on tight and I can nearly touch her. She starts cooing softly when I get within a few inches. I found a second moose cow with a single calf. Also, tracks of a hunting grizzly bear passing through.

Looking for bear

Twin Lakes
July 5, 1985

Dear Doris and Florence,

This book—have you read it? It was sent to me by one M. R." Whitey" Mohr of Seattle, and he wrote, "no need to return it." *"The Singer"* is a strange name for a book, I thought—a lot of unused paper, too. I started to read, and the farther I got, the more I thought it would be nice to listen to a good reader read it aloud—one who writes poetry could do it justice, I think. I read it through, and again, and part of it a third time. I feel sure that you girls will enjoy it—if you haven't read it before. Please keep it if you wish.

"The Singer" gives you the feeling of a song being sung, or at least it did me. I would be interested with your impression. I think you must understand it fully. Sincerely, Dick

TWIN LAKES
OCTOBER 23, 1985

Dear Doris and Florence,

There are traces of blue overhead and the thermometer reads ten degrees. It is snowing—a real nice calm-air snow. I wanted to go look for a real fancy white-cape bull caribou that –along with his smaller buddy—is spending some time along this upper lake. Never have I seen such good bulls here at rutting time, and I would like to study their habits. I'm writing letters to go—but when is very uncertain. It is most certain to be after freeze-up and that is a month and weeks away.

It was good of Mark to fly me to Nondalton, and I'm sorry we couldn't stay longer. About the deadline for getting back, I'm not sure for I saw no need for it when we got back. Lee, Mark and Mark's camp cook Alison brought me in. Lee, a student pilot, was in the driver's seat.

Florence, I'm sorry you had Post Office duty for the day, or at least that we couldn't stay and have lunch (the four of us.) Doris, I have one cookie left, and the bread is frozen up in the cache. It will be good for the holidays. Thank you for everything. I know you gave me every cookie in the house, and the bread came from the Co-op Store.

The visit to the Doll Factory was interesting, and I hope Nondalton works at making it pay—and a real credit to the community. I think those dolls—such as the one given me—are nice. I would like for my sister Florence in Iowa to have a few, so I am enclosing a check for fifty dollars. Would you please—if it is no problem—purchase twenty dollars (plus or minus) worth of dolls and mail them to my Sis. Make it twenty-five for dolls and postage. The remaining twenty-five is for you to spend as you see fit. Because you gave me cookies and bread, I would like to see you buy provisions to make Christmas treats for the little ones that are such good friends. OK?

Doris, did I hear you correctly about your T. V.? Did you say you could use it to run video tapes for the children or whoever? Would you have use for the video tape "*One Man's Alaska?*" I can get one— and would like the Mission to have one. I think you must have visitors from Outside who haven't seen the film. Or would you rather have the show on 16mm film? I think the video tape would be more convenient. If you can use one, please let me know the type your equipment uses—there are two kinds, I understand.

I have been cutting wood and thinking of you girls and your wood. Wish you lived close so we could get you up a pile of wood, too. The big wind storm (while I was at Port Alsworth) put many trees down here. I have them—seven—about cleaned up, and the last one is real good solid-white wood.

I have about five inches of snow here at lake level, and the low temperature to date is zero degree. The bear has gone in, I guess. About one week ago, I was on the mountain across to see the tracks of a mother and small cub. She had started a den but didn't suit, I guess, for they continued on up country. A *single* bear track went that way also.

I saw very few water fowl passing after my return October 7th. I can't believe they passed while I was at Port Alsworth, for that would be very early and little or no cold weather.

Just a few days ago I saw a loon still here, and I was surprised. Loons should have gone much earlier.

I've seen tracks of a wolf, wolverine, martin, lynx-cat, fox and ermine in the snow—until now. No rabbits yet, for they are at low cycle. Who makes the most tracks these days? The porcupine does pretty good, and of course the red squirrels.

The Park Service left a walkie-talkie with me for the winter. I can talk to the pilot if conditions are such that they can't land. Later, I can advise them of ice conditions—when they come after freeze-up. Hollis was by a few days ago to report no snow at Port Alsworth, and the temperature 18 degrees. I had 5 degrees that morning.

Now at noon, lots of blue and the lake noisy and rough. Snowing has ceased. Its winter-white all around—and I like it. After all, isn't winter the best time of all? Flo would agree.

Wishing you two—and your many friends—the best of health and a real nice holiday season. Thank you again for everything. Always my best, Dick Proenneke

TWIN LAKES
DECEMBER 7,

1985—2:40 P.M.

Dear Doris and Florence,

The days are getting short. Already the light is failing. It makes a long evening and night, so I usually take a three-or-four-mile walk before supper. It is 24 degrees with a wind down the lake today. The sky is only partly cloudy—as if it might clear for the night—one thing for sure, it can't get cold as long as the wind blows from the gulf.

Hollis and Ranger Christopher came with my mail December 2nd. This makes the 3rd time for them this fall. Have you met Chris? He is tall and handsome with a little mustache; by tall I mean more than six feet by quite a bit. He has trouble with my cabin door. The radio is a Motorola HT 440 I believe. I only use it to talk to Hollis about landing conditions here. I promised him a new cub if he broke through—so my mail could come pretty high (price-wise.)

Thank you, girls, for the big care package and the letter. More Irish potato bread and I still had the 1st loaf frozen in the cache. I have since started to use it. It is better than Co-op bread—to me. That fruit cake looks pretty as a picture, and is on hold until Christmas—along with the box of cookies. I was going to sample them, and found you had sealed the can. Everything sealed must wait. I am wearing that plush-velvet—or whatever—today for the first time. It is warm and oh so soft. The color might look better on you than me, but color is no problem, really. All this kindness is good, but I sent the check to buy ingredients to make cookies for the little guys of Nondalton. Yes, I know they received them. I wish about a dozen of them could come to help me eat the goodies and treat the three robbers. Seems to me I got my money back and with interest no less.

Regarding *The Singer,* I'm glad you liked it. Really not poetry, but the words do sort of fall in place now and then. I'm glad it found an appreciative home with that teacher, and it is hers from here to the bitter end as far as I am concerned. I shall report to *Whitey* in Seattle that his book found a home. I don't know too much about *Whitey*. He read my book and has been writing for years. He seems to be a salesman—a representative for many companies. He travels a lot—east, west, to Hawaii, Texas, Canada and Alaska. It seems I am living the way he wishes he was, and to write and hear from me sort of brings the wilderness life a little closer.

A letter came from my Sister, Florence. She was really thrilled with that Eskimo doll—as she called it. Are they considered Eskimo? I thought Athabascan maybe, but the features are more Eskimo than Indian—agree? Anyway, she does have a doll collection and will be happy with your choice. Perhaps she will have enough from Alaska to trade with friends.

I'm writing to my brother Robert in Arlington, VA. It is in Washington D. C. that the video tape is made of *One Man's Alaska*. I wasn't sure of the price, so I am sending him a signed check; he can fill in the amount. I asked him to mail the video to Florence and Doris—The Mission Girls, and if they write back wanting to pay, simply answer "There is no charge." I consider you girls two of the best—if not the very best—friends I have ever had, and it is my pleasure to furnish the tape for your enjoyment—and that of your friends. Have I made myself clear?

Florence, you wrote of dead birch for wood. Birch rots quickly. Do hope it hasn't been dead too long. Here, I have no birch, I thought. I did stumble onto a clump of three—and wouldn't you know, porcupines found them a little later and peeled all three—one beyond recovery, and I cut it. The other two were somewhat alive last time I saw them.

I don't think I ever wrote that I did write to Alaska Magazine and reported the Mission Girls had been here, finally. A letter came from the editor in Anchorage thanking me and saying Alaska would let the readers of *One Man's Wilderness* know that you had been to Twin Lakes. She wrote a top executive had dropped in about the time my letter arrived. He read it and was very pleased. He took it back to Edmonds, WA for the crew there to read. Until now, I haven't seen any mention of you two being to Twin Lakes. R. L. P.

Proof! Flo behind the camera?

We had a great time at Twin Lakes. We fed the birds, ate from Dick's bean-pot, and posed for Glen's borrowed video camera! The next morning was a great orange-red sunset, and Doris grabbed the camera and filmed it from her upstairs window! Since Flo was on the *other* end of the house looking out of *her* upstairs window. Had she seen Doris, she could have stopped me from wiping out all that documented proof: visiting the cabin and feeding the birds!

Twin Lakes
December 17

—MERRY CHRISTMAS—from my cabin to yours!

No snow to record the first fifteen days, and the average morning temperature—25 degrees. Last night two and a half inches of feather-light snow came during dead-calm. It is clearing now at 11 A.M. and beautiful. It was a real nice—though short—summer I had, and think you must have seen 45 to 50 degrees—40 degrees the high here, but nearly ten days of no freezing. Do you realize that today, the 17th, sees the earliest sunset? December 28th sees the latest sunrise. I'm looking forward to those stretching days. It's about January 5th that I start to notice the later sunset.

That was sad to hear of the two ducks trapped in the ice. I hadn't thought it possible that ducks would sit still long enough to let the ice grab them.

Here, my two caribou have stayed close. I saw them two days ago. They were becoming quite gentle with me checking on them most every day. I noticed November tenth that the bull had lost his impressive rack. That's early. Hollis reported at that time he was seeing many bull caribou jostling each other with big racks.

Sheep never had it so good—mild weather and less snow on the mountains than after the first snow of September. The wind scoured the mountains of snow.

On moose survey, Hollis and Chris counted 127 moose below the lower lake outside the park boundary—but in the preserve. They won't shed antlers until after the New Year is under way. I see tracks of the martin and of wolverine running in packs—a few rabbit tracks after none for a year or two. A red fox comes by now and then. Guess you know, the wilderness is always the same, but always different and always interesting.

Did you read in Alaska Magazine (guess you don't receive it) a little school girl wrote to this effect, "People write too much. When they come to a good place to stop, they should stop and end there." That is good advice, and it applies to me more often than not.

Plane day will be before Christmas. I do hope you get this before then so I can wish you a real nice

Christmas—and the wish goes to all of your many friends wherever they may be. May you enjoy the best of health, and may 1986 be especially good to you. Sincerely, Dick Proenneke

TWIN LAKES
APRIL 5, 1986

Dear Doris and Florence,

Remember April 10th of 1985? It was 20 degrees colder than today, but much, much nicer—the wind blowing about 25-30 and the temperature zero degrees. It is chilly to say the least. Glen A. is due any time now. We had scheduled last Saturday as the day, but no show. Then, I figured *this* Saturday would be plane day, but I wouldn't want him to come today.

It has been a long time since I wrote, and longer since I heard from the Mission Girls. Thought perhaps they had gone south or to Hawaii this past winter. Guess you heard, Glen V. bought a good-size forty-foot sail boat over there. That will be reason enough for him to go back again and again—even though he told me "Oh, I don't know, I'm not all that interested in Hawaii anymore."

By now you must have the video tape of *One Man's Alaska*. My brother Robert wrote they at last got it made and he sent it insured. He had called them, placing the order December 31st. But the paper-work said the order was received January 15th, and there would be four to six weeks delivery time. It comes from a government organization, and they claim to have 13,000 titles on hand. So perhaps they are pretty busy—which doesn't sound quite right. Anyway, I hope it came, and that it is a real good quality suited to your equipment.

How did your winter go? Bet you didn't have enough snow to go sledding. Glen A. came on skis one-time and said he just put them on, but didn't have enough snow on the runway to protect his skis. He was using Babe's Bay.

Here counting the days from October when the first zero weather came. I made this morning the sixty-four days of zero or below. Forty-six days since January 1st, 1986. There was eighty inches of snowfall which came before February 8th, and only a trace since that date. That's a long time with no snow. In the woods it has been about 18-19 inches for a long time. Sheep never had it so good. There is very little snow up there due to lots of wind every time it snowed.

December, January and until February 12, it was tropical with averages for the month being 26 degrees—and one two-week period in December had a 28 degree morning average. My winter came after mid-February for twenty-one days of minus twenty-one, morning-temperature-average. The whole of February had a morning average of less than one degree above zero, and March had an average of less than one degree below zero. The coldest reading for the winter was minus forty—that was February 27th and 28th. The lake ice was thirty-seven inches as of March 31st.

Having a very small snowshoe hare population, I had no great-horned owls, and I saw only a few Lynx cat tracks. A wolverine made many tracks, and I have a resident red fox that comes often. I only have one robber bird, and for what reason? I really have no idea. All three were here the day before Easter, which was a very windy day, and about zero—like today. Next day, only one came. Two days later, a second one came, but only once. Do you suppose they have kicked the welfare habit?

I feel that my ptarmigan population is coming back—after being low for quite a few winters. Sometime back—up the lake and the river—I flushed a flock that may have numbered about one hundred birds.

About a week ago—Easter morning, I feel quite sure—three wolves went up the shoreline across. I was over and saw their tracks, and back-tracked them a mile. The following day I went over to take some pictures of an unusually large track. I learned they had come back down on the same trail. When they came to my tracks, they promptly quit the trail and entered the timber—not returning to the lake again.

In zero weather, I made a plaster cast of the large track (6 inches long, 5 ¼ inches wide,) but of course the cast froze solid before it had time to set, so when it thawed it would be butter-soft or butter-warm. So with the frozen cast I made an imprint in a mixture of sawdust, flour, water and plaster of Paris. I dried it over the stove, and I think it is very nice—wish you could see it. It measures 6X51/4 inches, and place your hand alongside—I think you would agree that wolf was not just an ordinary bear!

This morning I cooked beans, finished the cast and wrote two letters—shoveled a little drifted snow, too.

All for now, and I hope this finds you two healthy and happy—as you always are. Have a real nice spring season. Come see my wolf track. Sincerely, Dick

"My sheep hear My voice, and I know them, and they follow Me. And I give them eternal life and they shall never perish; neither shall anyone snatch them out of My hand." John 10:27-28

TWIN LAKES
NOVEMBER 29, 1986

Dear Florence and Doris,

Storming fierce this afternoon, and I am writing a batch to go—come freeze-up. The lower lake closed up November 21st, and this one started to ice the 26th—but then the wind blew South East and spoiled it all—warming to 30 degrees. It is just now getting with the freeze-up program again. It is zero degrees at 2:30 A. M. Last night there were five inches of snow with wind; no more than a total of seven inches for this fall season.

Thank you, Florence, for your letter of August 7. Glad you two had a good trip out and back. The best news was that your check-up was just one more and no problem.

Maybe you heard that I did get flown out to harvest spuds, grade the runway, gravel Hollis and Pam's freeway and work for Dave Wilder and Governor Jay. *Skilled and respected Pilots have lived around Port Alsworth, and the Lake Country.*

Dave is one of the Best! How blessed we have been. (See This Side of the Past—Alaska's Port Alsworth. Volume I). I was just finishing one and starting the next—until it was time to climb aboard for the flight back. Again in October I made a short two-day trip out to help Dave with his John Reindeer loader. *John Reindeer* is Chuck and Sara's granddaughter's name for Chuck's *John Deere.*

Good to hear that your garden did well this time. Glen didn't get the potato crop of last year, due to a big wind exposing the seed after planting—then dry too long. Good rain finally got the program going, and the one half of the patch that is always best came pretty good—maybe 3000 pounds of spuds, and pretty nice and smooth for size.

The blueberry crop wasn't the greatest this time, but enough for the wild bunch and me. Just very, very few blossoms in June—and that was a first. Usually there are scads of bloom but few berries— due to not being pollinated, I suppose. Anyway, I had buckets—six-pound peanut-butter containers— in stock for a few weeks.

Bet you had good fall colors this time. It is really nice here—good weather for being *overcast.* I like blue sky and sunshine for my fall color pictures.

Do you know Alison W. who cooked at Mark and Sandi's last year—and for Chuck and Sara this season? Hollis dropped her off here for four days. I opened Spike's cabin for her sleeping quarters, and she had her meals with me. I enjoyed her company a lot—a strong hiker, good with a canoe, liked to pick blueberries and a good cook. She turned twenty-five the second day here. We celebrated by picking two buckets of berries—hand-picked, they looked nice in a yellow peanut-butter bucket. We had a fire in the fireplace after supper and played tapes of old time hit tunes. I missed her after she flew away, and hope she comes again sometime. I wish that you two could arrange to come—for a few days at least. I would turn my cabin over to you, and me sleep in Spike's cabin. You could build the morning fires, get breakfast and feed the triplets: Jasper, Jenny and Junior—the robbers by name.

I saw two wolverine several times this fall, and pretty close a couple times. A bull moose drowned in the lake. A grizzly bear dragged him ashore and had his fill. The wolverines were there daily. Two eagles, ravens, magpies and camp-robbers helped to clean up the remains, of which there are now very few.

About the usual thirty-five to forty head of sheep on the mountain—and maybe ten to twelve rams—some real nice ones. Where do they summer? I have about six to ten head on this side from spring to fall, and I wonder if they cross over above the lake and winter on the north side.

About eighty-five people signed my guest book this last season. Because I have my own time, sun time, God's time—I am two hours later than Port Alsworth. I would sometimes no more than have breakfast out of sight, and the cabin and area scented up—when Glen V.'s beaver-plane arrives with loads of visitors. It was the Audubon Society of Maine last year and this—real nice people, and I wish for more from back east.

Denmark, France and Switzerland were represented. From the Danes I learned that doc is a dog. I thought the man meant *boat doc when he really said, "why no doc?"* From the Swiss I learned that I am living in a hut. When I met them three miles down, the first question was, *"Where is your hut?"* Good hikers, those old country natives.

So now, my wood is in close. I put a new moss covering on my roof last summer, and it is doing real well. After I put it on I watered it heavy until the rains came. It produced some crow berries, and the small fireweed didn't even wilt. Imagine—a self-repairing roof!

The first half of November had a 33.2 degree morning average temperature. October was mild also. I saw no bears on the move as if heading for winter quarters. In the past I have seen bears still traveling at Thanksgiving time, but not often.

Now, I'm not sure when plane day will be. Glen has wanted to come by helicopter, and mentioned near Thanksgiving—but it was minus 19 then, and I didn't expect him. Now, I expect, it will be after freeze-up, which can come anytime it calms. It is zero degrees now, at 3:15 P.M.

I'll close for now, shovel my snow, pack wood and water, and call it a pretty good day. I do hope that this finds you two healthy and just as happy as you always seem to be. Hope you had a real nice Thanksgiving—and that Christmas will be especially nice. Hello and best wishes to Pete and Ruth, your faithful neighbors. My best to you always, Dick Proenneke

Homemade and hand-hewn

TWIN LAKES
DECEMBER 9TH

Where has the winter gone? Temperature was plus 30 degrees this morning, and the sun was very high on the solid-white mountain across. It rained here, and snowed up there last night. Still, there is no ice on this lake. It tried three times — but each time, that south-east wind came to spoil it all. Maybe during the coming December 16th full moon, suppose? R. L. P.

Twin Lakes
January 11, 1987

Dear Doris and Flo

Oh you kids! There should be a bumper sticker reading "I love the Mission Girls!" Thank you for the Christmas-gift care package. The two little loaves of bread are not keeping worth a cent. The teapot that you hug with both hands—I don't know the proper name or its intended use, but I think it will be a great teapot when I get a beaver-load of tourists. And thanks, too, for your nice note and *Our Daily Bread.*

It was Christmas all over again when Hollis came on January 8th with more mail than Glen flew in by copter on December 17th. The total score: about 100 cards and letters plus sixteen parcels—no one here to read and appreciate them but me and the wild bunch. I did have seven moose—one a real nice bull, and gentle. Freeze-up came on Christmas Day—a real nice gift, for I had been trying to get this lake iced over since Thanksgiving. The lower lake closed up on November 21st. This one tried three times, but always the wind came warm and blew for days. I put the canoe in storage on November 26th.

December 28th a big wolverine came to my window as I sat reading by the lantern light: I heard snow crunching, and wondered if it was a moose passing on the beach. It kept coming closer, and I expected to see someone's face at the window. Then it went towards the front. I went with flashlight, expecting to see eyes shining into the light. From alongside the cabin moved a big wolverine. At eight feet, he stood looking at the light—not a bit spooked. As he turned broadside, you could see his beautiful coat. He went slowly down the path and on down the lake. That was something to make you hold your breath—and your heart beat in your throat. Never have I seen a wolverine so bold as that.

Hasn't this been some winter? No winter, really, until night before last, and minus 43 degrees. It was never warmer than minus 40 yesterday. It was minus 25 degrees this morning, and at noon the wind came. Now at 2:00 P.M. Clear, wind down the lake and 16 degrees. Sheep country has been nearly snow-free, due to wind, since snows came to stay. Here in the woods, maybe sixteen inches of snow, and on the lake, six inches of ice.

It's good to have the days stretching. Today, sunlight touched the ice on the far side. February 1ˢᵗ it will be here—then full speed ahead to the long days. Imagine how it must be to live without the two long seasons and the two very short ones. Give me Alaska's four.

I'm pleased that you enjoy *Alaska Magazine*. I remembered you saying that you didn't receive that magazine. I think it is pretty nice, and its writing very popular. Wasn't it nice that the 82-year-old Florida lady dreamed of spending some time in Alaska—and her dream is coming true. Too bad countries around the world can't be as kind and thoughtful of each other.

Closing for now and I'm wishing you—the Mission Girls—the best of health for 1987. May you find a minute to come visit Twin Lakes for a few days or a week this blueberry-picking time. I intend to tell Glen, "Tell the Mission Girls they have just won a free vacation to *One Man's Wilderness*." So, plan with that in mind. My best wishes always, Dick Proenneke.

P.S. Four camp robbers come knocking at my door these days. R. L. P.

TWIN LAKES
MARCH 19, 1987

Dear Doris and Florence,

I have just sampled my latest batch of poor man's chili—not chili, really, but close. Hmm! Not bad! Wish you were here to join me.

Outside it is pretty white and twenty degrees—12 degrees early and minus 2 degrees yesterday morning. I have a plane coming on Saturday the 21st—first day of spring, no? My calendar isn't marked. I haven't had mail since February 13th—when Lee came in his Tri-Pacer. He said, "I'm just trying to learn how to fly the thing, and thought I would come up." It was a beautiful day, and the lake ice perfect for wheels.

Thank you for your good letter of February 3rd—along with your form-letter telling of the breakdown of the Mission Girls. 1986 was just not a good year for girls, I guess. In the same mail with yours, my Sister Florence wrote of two of her friends taking a tumble and crippled up. One broke her glasses, nose and sprained an ankle pretty severely. The other was using that good product *Pledge* and slipped on her own polishing spill. Voight and Sis were here last Saturday the 14th and reported both of you out of the woods—and Babe's Mary getting around, and their daughter Sis thinking she will return to normal.

Since your letter, I have been thinking about a young pilot with passenger landing for gas. He was from a village, and starting an air service. Was it he who crashed—and for what reason? Weather, no doubt. Has everyone recovered pretty well? Were there some bad injuries?

I suspected your gift-container might be for bacon grease, though I had never seen one. Boy, it would hold a lot—but not much the way Babe and Mary used to fry bacon. A large pan of it in the oven, and Mary sent grease to me by the half-gallon. You wrote, "We seldom have bacon" and that fits me, too. I do try to keep some on hand for seasoning my pinto beans. Just this last Christmas season, I decided to splurge a bit. L. L. Bean had three pounds of corn-cob-smoked bacon for $12 postpaid. Boy, that's a lot, I thought, but just once—and I had never tasted corn-cob smoked. They didn't like to mail it outside the lower 48—thinking it too far and might spoil. I requested they send it and I would take the chance. It came in perfect condition and priority mail—which they paid ($5.88.) It is very good. (Yes, I still have a pound—for like you, I don't have bacon often.)

I do use bacon grease on my griddle and some for shortening in my small loaves of sourdough bread. I keep the grease in a peanut-butter can with plastic cover. The container works for a cookie jar, and will be good for tea when the tourists come.

In February (for three weeks) I had close neighbors, Garry and Christina of Sterling, who bought two acres of deeded land across the lake—and came to see Twin Lakes in winter. We hiked and climbed a lot. They stayed in a cabin on a hill near here, and invited me for supper. I invited them for beans and a hotcake breakfast. They were a real nice, young couple with a golden retriever dog. He is my friend. I dropped a mitten high on the mountain, and it went down, down and still sliding. Ryan saw it go, and down the mountain he went—fetching it to me. We shared my lunch. When they flew away, they left me several packages of moose burger; that's where I got the burger for my chili. This morning, Voight and Sis brought a half gallon of vanilla ice cream. I buried it in a snow bank, and it has kept prctty well—but one more serving with butter-scotch-fudge topping will see it gone. (smile!)

My winter was a sissy one until now—snowing big flakes. The low was minus 43 degrees in early January, and after, only one night with a minus 25 degree. Then late February and six days of March saw ten days of clear and calm, with a morning average of minus 22 degrees and minus 29 degrees the low. Snowfall until now was about sixty inches, with twenty inches of snow in the woods. Lake ice was 28 inches, and not much snow on the ice. It would be good for wheels.

I do hope you girls are getting around like girls these days—must have looked sad to see you both limping! Here, about the same. No problem. Dick

We had ordered new shoe-pacs, same size as always, but a narrow-topped, thinsulated style. Flo had hers on when she went to the shop-building to get the three-wheeler. Some folk needed a lift to the airstrip, and it was glare ice outside. Flo's feet went out from under her, and down she went. She called for my help, but sadly I couldn't hear her. Perhaps the light-plant was running (noisy.) She crawled up onto the Honda three-wheeler and proceeded to get the folk up to the airstrip. The flight was cancelled, so she came back home. I finally realized her plight, and helped her into the house. Her foot was swelling, and I new her boot had to come off. We did get the boot off, but Flo's ankle was swelling to the point of "broken?"

Flo was air-lifted to Anchorage, where she received a plaster-cast on foot. She stayed in town with Loren and Pam Kroon until she was able to return. Meanwhile, Doris forced her own new boots off—and ended up with foot-problems for the rest of her years. We did write a nice letter to the boot-company, and they graciously took that boot out of their catalog. We respected them for that, and they remained a favorite company and most popular! They refunded each of us a new pair of boots that fit, and we wore them for years.

Voight Clum and Dick
The find of a moose-antler!

TWIN LAKES
SEPTEMBER 23, 1987

Dear Florence and Doris,

Greetings from the land of new snow (on peaks and ridges)—and from the land of the tardy one. Many times I noticed your good letter of May 19th— as I shuffled my stack of letters to answer, and many times I didn't get with the program and write.

Today, I have been busy, busy. Word came in that Jay Hammond was coming with a video crew for an interview—something about interesting people, as I got it. I really gave this diggins a neatening up. Even swept the leaves from the pathways, screened gravel and touched up the bare spots, raked the beach and briefed my robbers about hamming for the camera— and nobody came. Have you ever wondered if little airplanes are here to stay? Seems half of my time is spent waiting for one. I hear the Park Service from Anchorage is due in tomorrow in a Goose, and they will have a video camera and recorder aboard. I should tell those program producers—as I did our local newspaper reporter back home after she finished asking questions and making notes—I said, "Now Sally, I don't mind you writing all this, but don't put it in the paper." She didn't.

So how has your summer gone since you got back from your June trip? Hope your garden was a good producer, and now the ground not too wet to dig spuds. Last spring I ordered my Sis Florence some material called *Ply ban row-cover*. It comes four feet wide and fifty feet long—very thin plastic and perforated with millions of tiny holes. Cover your rows and load the edges with a little dirt. Rain goes through, and the ground is warmer due to the greenhouse effect. It keeps the pests out. She reports that potatoes under it did better, and tomatoes did very good. It was $8 for the fifty feet. I am enclosing the information. I think I could grow something here by using it. Grouse and rabbits always got green stuff, and frost in July flattened my potatoes. Rhubarb does best, and one year, twin moose calves ate the leaves of it.

Your ice went out on May 11th, and mine on the 30th. Snowfall for the season was sixty inches—against eighty last year, and one-hundred-sixty the year before. Lake ice is about thirty inches.

New lambs started May 10th—five or six more real soon after. The crop was about twenty to twenty-two. The first moose calves—twins—on May 24. I saw several, and had a run-in with a blond bear that was after a little moose-calf. It swam and the bear followed. The calf circled back to me on the beach. Lots of shouting and throwing rocks turned the bear aside as they were coming closer. That little calf—ears drooping and on trembling legs—was nearly helpless, but it could holler for its mom, and she came. It followed her away on very wobbly legs—while I stood guard expecting the bear to try again. I never saw the bear or its tracks again.

The blueberry crop was a near complete failure this time—lots of blossoms, but a strong nine-day wind that kept the insects down, if they are the pollen spreaders. There were good showers all summer, and you must have had them too. Fishing was not as productive as last year, and my red run was weak too.

In early August I had two *birders* here from Rhode Island. Because they refer to that tiny state as *little Rhody*, I made them the *Little Rhody Girls*. Both were teachers. I wish you could have seen them working at *birding*. They were fast to spot and identify birds—even birds new to them. With binoculars, they were experts. A couple mornings, I had them out on the creek flat glassing a grizzly and counting thirty-two head of caribou bulls. Guess you know my robbers got pampered and talked to as if they were first graders.

My resident fox pair had four puppies. Being acquainted with me, they didn't mind me at the den. I heard—on two occasions—the vixen called the pups, and these times I saw food come to the den. A big rabbit was packed in. It was a terrible fight by the pups to see who ate first. Pup number two fought pup number one, and pup number three fought pup number 2. Pup number four fought pup three for the remains. Each had to fight the one feeding for its share. Me and two-toes—the father fox—watching the show. I was sick for taking the still camera and 8X lens instead of the movie camera that day.

Fourteen degrees the fourteenth of September froze the leaves too much I'm expecting to go harvest spuds about this coming Saturday the 26th, but Glen may wait a week. You probably haven't heard from Glen that you won a free trip to Twin Lakes—due to the fact I haven't told him yet. I have seen him only one time since I wrote to you about it, and I forgot to tell him then. Next time, I promise—cross my heart. I won't forget. I won't forget.

End of the paper and light failing. Wishing you two the very best—and have a nice Thanksgiving. Here, about the same, Dick

Tanalian Mountain and Port Alsworth potato patch
– a new generation!

Hungry Fox?

Twin Lakes
September 17, 1990

—42 degrees—raining and calm

Dear Doris and Florence,

I'm digging out. It was a spring and summer like no other. There were days and weeks of fine weather—no rainy season until recently—then the lake rose up past the shoreline, into the brush. It's too late to make sheep-feed on the mountain, and I'm concerned about their winter feed being in very short supply. It was the first time for me to see dried blueberries on the bush. Some were shriveled dry—more so than raisins. Even patches of brush and tundra suffered; leaves turned and moss looked dry.

It was a summer for hikers, campers and river floaters—with a good number of all three. Some floaters had no floating experience. A few days ago, there was word of an over-turned raft—where the Chilly enters the Mulchatna—and a helicopter was urgently needed. Leon and Joe flew and dropped a note, "If you are okay, sit down." "If you must come out, stand up." Next pass showed them standing and waving their arms. Another hunting party sent word of a heart attack. A dedicated pilot was able to air-lift the hunter to Anchorage on time. (The two hunters with known heart conditions were fine, but the healthy hunter had the heart attack.)

Me? No big problem other than lots of mail stack-up. I missed a bunch, but still have more than eighty names in my new guest book. The Providence, R. I. birder-lady came again for ten days. I always give her my cabin, and I move to Spikes up on the point. We searched and picked blueberries for a triple batch of jam for winter hot cakes. It was so warm—near eighty. While picking on a south-facing steep bank, she felt light headed. We took a break for lunch in the shadow of a spruce.

Just a few days ago—as I was declaring revile—Mark Lang came with three Homer friends. One had been here several years ago and wanted to visit a few minutes. They had seen the Park Service Movie "One Man's Wilderness," and wanted to see it in reality. Another man came, Howard E. from New Jersey. He chartered Bill D. and his Otter (plane) from Homer.

All that is past now, and I am writing letters. I surely do thank you girls for your letter and books mailed back about July 22nd. The Bible Dictionary is of great interest to me. I really enjoy it. You are certainly right—know the dictionary, and you understand better. It answers many more questions than reading the Old or the New Testament by themselves—or at least it does for me. I did read the One Year Bible through—Old and New Testaments—then realized that to read one at a time was better for me. So now I am to August 20th of the Old Testament. A Bible was sent to me years and years ago, but sorry to say, it is in mint condition.

You know, I leaf through the dictionary and it leads me to wonder if it was or is a very in-hospitable land—certainly not one of milk and honey—but there must be some very fertile land, much livestock, grapes and olives, very dry and rocks no end. Have either of you ever visited the area? I wonder if living conditions have changed a lot since then. It seems most everyone lived in a tent and went bare footed—or wore sandals, at best. Gold! I'm surprised at the amount—and silver and bronze. And where did the gold come from? Igor, wasn't it? In south Arabia—three years travel away! I wonder if a lot of gold has been found in recent diggings—for artifacts?

Questions and curiosity about Israel's temple, its gold—and some of the building stones weighing over 400 tons—peaked Dick's interest in reading the Bible. He read where one of the disciples said to Jesus, "what wonderful stones and what wonderful buildings!" Jesus replied, "Do you see these great buildings? Not one stone will be left upon another which will not be torn down." Jesus declared predictions were and are correct. When the temple area was captured in 70 A.D, a fire had engulfed the structure causing the gold and silver of the temple to melt and flow between the cracks of the stone. History tells us Soldiers pried apart the massive stones to get to the great supply of gold. Not one stone was left standing upon another.

Here, my camp-robbers come monthly any more—to be sociable. I don't see them for days—then suddenly here they are—all three! I feed them, and away they go again! Maybe this winter will put them in the welfare mood. A real nice bull caribou walked by a few mornings ago. He was round as a ball with winter fat—travelling the beach—antlers brown and polished. No lambs in a bunch of more than fifty sheep at the mineral lick in mid-June. Last winter was too stressful, I think. Fishing has been good—a 23 ¾ inch Lake Trout was my best. Wish you could sample Lake Trout—Twin Lakes style! I must close for now, wishing you two the best of health. Thank you for everything. Sincerely, Dick

TWIN LAKES
JANUARY 21, 1991

—25 degrees—blowing snow—1 P.M.

To the Mission Girls at McAdoo Way—

Dear Doris and Florence,

Usually I clear snow first thing after breakfast, and here it is after noon, and still the snow shovel hangs unused. The reason: snow and more snow coming down—and after five inches yesterday. Thirteen days of snow in November—fifteen inches of it. Is this out to beat the record?

It's a good day to write a batch of letters. With twenty-two to twenty-three packages at Christmas time—along with my usual writing load—I am trying to get a thank you to all those good people who thought of me. Really, I wish they would not be so generous. Soxs! I received several pair, but must admit, no white ones, and certainly not a testimonial to end all. The poet of the Mission Girls team did it again, and I wonder just how many minutes it took to come up with those lines???

The box came in January 4th—with Leon in the Park Service Super-Cub—no postage, no return address, and in fact, no names at all—just in-care-of *Lake Clark Air*. So there was no doubt. I certainly do thank you girls for everything, including the calendar. That little foil-wrapped loaf-cake is lasting remarkably well. Good things are rationed severely at Twin Lakes. Fig bars! Now there is an old timer that hasn't changed over the years, and is always good. I have a batch of popcorn; I haven't sampled the grapes and cherries as yet.

How are you girls, and how is the weather up there? The poor moose, I hope they are not buried in snow again. Due to three to four nights of rain at Christmas time, my thirty-inch snow pack went down to twenty-two inches, but this storm may build it back. Snow has not been a real problem for moose, but a pack of eleven wolves may cause them considerable pain. Four big grey ones and seven blacks—which is a lot of black wolves. It looked like a kennel of Labrador's coming single-file up the shoreline as I sat thinking. I'm not afraid of a wolf—or two or three—but *eleven*! I wasn't really afraid, I just knew that I wasn't in command. At their closest, the big, grey leader and a black the same size, were not one hundred feet from me across the stream between the lakes—me sitting against a bank with binocular to my eyes.

They stood looking at me, but it didn't register, and they moved down stream to cross to my side. They left without ever seeing me and realizing their most feared enemy was so close. Next day I went back down to track them and see if they took a moose. A mile on the trail and there were a few remains of a caribou bull. Very little was left after the eleven ate their fill.

An interesting site it was—to see the bull's antlers had dropped at the site and separated from the skull in a natural, dropped-antler fashion. So, late October sees caribou bulls ready to drop antlers. Moose don't until January or February.

The wolf-pack disappeared. Park Service flew moose survey and didn't see a wolf or a moose kill site. Then came Leon to say he saw the pack at Snipe Lake—a cow and calf moose, the calf dead. The pack was lying in a circle around them, waiting. Next check found only a few heavy bones, and no cow or the pack. How often will the pack make a kill? I think it will take more than one moose a week to keep them satisfied. Rather sad, I think, but that's nature. Something dies every day so something can live.

Again, this last mid-October I found a nice big dark grizzly at a fresh-dug den, and I can—with the scope—see the den from here. October 17th was the last day, and will the record of 197 days under the snow be broken by this last day? It worked until last light that last day—raking grass for a bed in the den. The last bear I watched rake den grass, came out with triplets come mid-April of the following year. Using *Sig's* words, "Is it only the Mother ones who rake grass?" Certainly, very few bears do.

It has been a pretty wild winter until now—lots of snow in a short time, and very early. Temperatures to 38 degrees at Christmas time; rain until the lake was flooded. Cold to fifty below zero, and for forty-eight hours—ice being made at the rate of eight inches in four days.

There were no new lambs last May, and not one lamb at the sheep lick in June. Now they are having another tough winter, and I expect the population to be down come flowers in May.

Another first for Twin Lakes: A pine martin came one bright day. I saw it climb spruce to about twenty-five feet, and then leap into space to land

and disappear in the deep snow. Twice it did the same, and I have seen sign of it in other places.

I think you must be wondering how I have been coming with my Bible reading. I read most of the Old Testament, and studied the dictionary a lot. It is very interesting. Laddy and Glenda sent me *Unfolding Daniel's Prophecies,* which was very interesting. One thing I did learn for sure was that there have been wars, wars, wars—from the very beginning. I wonder if any country today could wage war so brutally. That big sword was certainly a common and much-used weapon. A period of peace and prosperity never failed to lead to a period of war. How many wars since the beginning, I wonder? How many millions have died by the sword??

If you read the paper, you wouldn't fail to miss the trials and tribulations of people's lives. All I can add is that I am very sorry it has to be that way. I wish that if I ignored it that it would go away.

I thought perhaps Leon would come today, as he is way past his intended arrival, but after the storm he must have bigger fish to fry first. I'll close this for now and get it ready to fly. Sometimes it's a rush when the planes come. All a pilot can think about while waiting is how far he can fly. So, thank you girls, again, for everything. Good health, good fortune—and may the year of 1991 be really good to you. My best always, Dick

TREASURED YEARS

Those Treasured Years of Christmas lie deep within
my heart
Where memories of loved ones and friends still
have their part
I think of all the blessings—God by His grace
bestowed
And treasured years of CHRISTMAS so freely
overflowed.

Remembered scenes of childhood—the family
gathered 'round
Fun food upon the table; fine carol-tunes abound
Bring tinsel, stars and stockings—string popcorn
on the scene
Hand-made the decorations in colors red and green.

Big snowflakes fall from heaven to blanket
earth below
We'd find a hill for sledding; make angels in
the snow

We sing *Come All Ye Faithful,* and then *O Christmas Tree*
Those treasured years of Christmas still mean so much to me.

Though memories may falter, there's one that will not die
It's written in the Bible—on history pages nigh
The story of a Savior, of wise-men travelling far
They seek for Christ-child Jesus, while following a star.

There Joseph, Mary, Jesus—I love the story true
Recorded with a timeline for Grandma, Grandpa, too
One day the story reached me, and in my heart I know
The Treasured Truth of Christmas has set my heart aglow.

I heard the church bells ringing, as people filled the pews
And anthems rose in singing—those hymns of God's Good News
About the Savior's birthday; His death on Calvary's tree
We sang the Resurrection; His Coming Back for me.

Now may this treasured memory—in spirit make us strong

May God's truth ne'er be tainted, nor smothered by man's wrong

Though some would quench the story, they cannot steal God's grace

And Christ, God's Word fulfilling, will one day show His face.

His love and peace enable—in Him we can confide

He knows our every moment; we never need to hide.

God holds our lives securely, forgives and makes man whole

Adopts us—we're His family! *Rejoice* and *Sing* my soul!

So, *stand true* to the Savior, and hold His story dear

This treasured truth of Christmas will keep your heart from fear

Christ Jesus IS the Treasure: THE WAY, THE TRUTH, THE LIFE

He fills our hearts forever—and shields from dismal strife.

Such Treasured Truth of Christmas still permeates the lands

His PRESENCE fills the faithful—and flows
toward open hands
Let's lead the way to JESUS—life's CHRISTMAS
TREASURE TRUE
For LORD, our LIFE ETERNAL is always found
in YOU.

dh 2008

Twin Lakes
November 18, 1991

—minus 10—fog—1:45 P.M.

Dear Doris and Florence,

I'm writing a batch of letters in the first below-zero day of the season. The weather was overdue—last year by now had a week of it with a low of minus 21. Not sure when my outgoing will fly, for November moon is the waiting moon: waiting for freeze-up and landing ice. As of November 15th, the lower lake has closed up. So, by now the ice is Cub-safe—but of course Leon doesn't know that. I will go down and check it and inform him by radio when he comes.

Thank you, girls, a lot for your parcel of June 19th. I enjoyed your letter, and now I have forgotten what—in the line of cookies—came for my birthday. It strikes me that my two sisters in Iowa sent me a shipment of caramel-corn. I request that when they ask, for it is easy to make, pack and travel—good over the long trail. Please don't feel bad about missing my birthday. Don't you agree that too many birthdays are our number one problem? If only we could start counting down instead of always higher. What did I do on my birthday? I will never forget. I had been training for a month, and it was a determined effort. Of course, you don't know about the Twin Lakes Olympics. Park Service holds theirs at Port Alsworth. They are good, but I think they would win no gold if they competed with me at my chosen events. There are a few, but one is special. For me, it is chin-the-bar seventy-five times—one for each year—feet flat on the deck, and one full breath between lifts. Chin the bar seventy-five times in ten minutes. For a week before my seventy-fifth, I was ready, and knew I could do it—although I hadn't done it. The afternoon of the seventy-fifth birthday, I chinned the bar eighty-five times by my system. So much for birthdays!

Although I hadn't heard from you all summer, Sis Clum kept me posted pretty well. Doris went outside for a week—as I remember. Florence held down this end, and is there a sizable lawn to mow? Garden is small, you wrote. So is mine, but I grew a round red radish that measured twelve and a half inches around the waist. The seeds came from England.

Thank you, too, for the *New International Version* of the *Holy Bible*. Now there is a Bible that reads pretty much like a good book, and I like that. A question: Who wrote the first paragraph of Genesis?

Response: The Bible is the Word of God in the words of man. II Timothy 3:16, 17 says "All Scripture is given by inspiration of God, and is profitable for doctrine, for reproof, for correction, for instruction in righteousness, that the man of God may be complete, thoroughly equipped for every good work." II Peter 1:21 says "prophecy never came by the will of man, but holy men of God spoke as they were moved by the Holy Spirit." God is Eternal—Three in One—Father, Son and Spirit. Scripture explains Scripture.

"...since the creation of the world His invisible attributes are clearly seen, being understood by the things that are made, even His eternal power and Godhead." Romans 1:20 Though God used Moses to write the first five books of the Bible, it was God who revealed the Scriptures to Moses. We are told Jesus Christ is the Living Word, John, Chapter1.

Thanks, too, for the lessons—though I doubt if I will ever get to them—lots and lots more of letters to answer. Some people bribe me with a shoebox of chocolate treats so I will write—due to feeling guilty for not writing. One pretty girl, a fishing lodge guest from California did that. She thinks if a lot more people lived as I do the world would be a better place to live—maybe for a little while. Remember, the strong dominate the weak. I feel you don't agree??

David, the Shepherd boy in the Bible, took down the Giant Goliath! David became King of Israel. His son was Solomon, who was given wisdom and riches more than any other king on earth. He inherited the gold and riches stored up by his father, David—who lead his armies to victory in the strength of the Lord. Isaiah 40:28, Romans 12:10. Isaiah 40:28-31 "those who wait on the LORD shall renew their strength; They shall mount up with wings like eagles, they shall run and not be weary, They shall walk and not faint."

Maybe we had better get back to Twin Lakes. The ice went out early in June. A nice spring-dry-season followed by a normal rainy season. I saw four grizzly bears early—one mother with new twins. A good lamb and moose calf crop, but again a grizzly got a calf right here close to home. Sometimes I think a tame cow will stay close, thinking I am protection from the bears—not so. A bear will run over me to get a calf.

Owners came from a lodge under new management—looking for good fishing holes and entertaining a few guests by bringing them here for a visit. Ninety-five people signed my guest-book this season. If the boat is driven too fast on rough water, it can be torture—the pounding jars the brain.

This was a blueberry year—best since 1975 at twin Lakes—big as grapes, I heard it said, and for some I guess it seemed so. Blue Berry Hill—two miles down this south side—has the big ones, and just blue in isolated small patches. It was a good season with no airplane accidents—but oh so close. One person turned his little red T-craft over on a gravel bar here between the lakes. He and I righted it. Now it sets—lonesome like—waiting for a prop that got bent but good.

Wish you two could have been here to see a good bull moose swim the lake when it was roaring rough. I could hardly see him out there, but in due time, he waded out on the far shore, and tired? Not at all!

I stood a good watch in October, but saw no bears denning on the far side. Last winter, two did, and the twin cubs came from one den.

Doris! I must not fail to mention your two poems. They were in good form, and I fail to see how you get the proper words following the first one.

End of page and light going. Surely do wish you girls the best of health and a very happy end-of-season holidays. A real nice Thanksgiving and Christmas followed by the best ever new year. Sincerely, Dick

P.S. I like your zip number. Makes you seem just over the mountain.

Twin Lakes
January 25, 1992

—Zero—calm—1 1:30 A.M.

Dear Doris and Florence,

Fine morning and it has been a very pleasant winter until now—minus 43 degrees, the low, with minus thirty-six and minus twenty-three next. Maybe seventy inches of snowfall, and twenty-five inches—the snowpack where there was no drifting. No rain and snow this snow season, and that's appreciated.

I'm sorry to be so late in thanking you girls for that super care package. Everything was very good, and when I look at those sox I think, "Bet you they are the best sox I have ever worn." I hate to put them into service—like to keep the best for a while. And the little book, *Our Daily Bread,* I enjoy and wonder if Babe still reads it mornings at the breakfast table? Someone saw him and Mary at the Air Terminal in Anchorage, and Babe said this was going to be his last trip to Alaska. I think Mary would be happy to move back permanently.

Leon recently brought in your care package. He remarked that it had been in the hangar quite a while. He hoped there was nothing in it that would spoil. The candies stood the test perfectly, but the cupcakes and loaf were showing some sign of white. On the loaf, I at first thought it was white glaze frosting, but then I noticed some on the bottom, too. A little mold is good for you, so with a table knife, I scraped it off for the robbers—no complaint. And the cupcakes, I had to trim a bit. They are gone, but I am still eating the loaf—which is stored in my storage space out front. Some blueberry jam on it makes real good cake with my dessert.

Here it has been a pretty quiet winter, with few visitors. Daniel stopped in a couple times with Christmas mail—coming to scrounge parts and the engine from a wind-totaled T-craft.

The highlight was the visit by my seventeen-pack. We are all familiar with six-packs, but this one was a super-pack. Seventeen wolves came to the upper lake and stayed a few days. On the Lake ice—directly across from here—they devoured a three-year-old cow moose. They were about equal as to color—blacks and greys. There were five or six this-year's-pups in the pack. There were some big old-timers, and they came to check me out when I went over to check the kill. One big grey came plenty close—for a killing shot with Leon's wolf mini 14 Rugger. Two days, they stayed and even came back to feed after I was there. I wish you could have heard the pack howl—which they did after I left the kill and for an hour or more. The mountains answered their howl, and so did I. All up and down the scale they went. I like to hear those big ones that howl loud and low.

It is something to see ravens and wolves feeding on a kill. Some wolves will tolerate ravens—to feed with them shoulder to shoulder. Others chase the ravens away, but it is a half-hearted chase—as if they wouldn't hurt them if they did catch one. Ravens on all sides, and when the wolf chases out from the kill, ravens behind will dart in and get a few bites before the wolf is back to chase those feeding. So, he can't win due to their teamwork. The ravens probably get about—or as much—meat as the wolf. When the wolf-pack left, so did the ravens. I think they do follow the pack, for they know there will be more fresh meat soon.

Leon and Andy came. The pack left a couple days later, seen near Pear Lake on their way here, and yes, they had made another moose kill. Leon and Joe came later, and they had searched and found the pack. They had a moose surrounded, and Leon thought it had been badly injured and was standing head down in shock. I hope Leon checks on the pack as often as he can—to learn first about how many moose a big pack needs to stay well-fed. It is interesting to track the big pack in semi-deep, six to eight inches of snow. They single file a lot. Sometimes—and quite often—all members of the pack will use the leader's tracks, and for maybe fifty feet or more. Seldom do they spread out, so you can tell exactly how many wolves there are. I started tracking when they came—maybe twelve or maybe only ten, then fifteen for sure, and after a couple miles, seventeen for sure.

I brought back the head, a part of front leg and a length of neck bone for my robbers. A red fox came, and now I have a pet. It comes nearly every day, and will sit patiently for me to chop some frozen meat and bone. Guess you know, the robbers don't give the fox any sass.

Hope you girls had a real good Christmas holiday season. Know that you did, for it is your nature to be an inspiration for all who come in contact.

Me, I was crippled for a while—sprained my left foot in the arch, and lucky for me, my seventeen and a half inches of snow had been shoveled before it disabled me. I crawled from my bunk to the stove for fire building a few mornings. Now, no problem; I have nearly recovered.

Closing and wishing you two the best of everything good. May '92 be the best ever year. Dick

P.S. Another question: In Heaven will the Mission Girls still make good cakes and candy??

I think they'd come pre-baked – smile!

Christmas comes around each year,
heartfelt Carols, songs of Cheer,
Colored lights and Tinseled tree
these reflect God's Love to me.
Cards and email, word from Friends,
bring us close as old year ends.
Year-long News and Pictures too,
these are Gifts of Kindness true!
Thank You for keeping in touch with us!
dh

Twin Lakes
February 3, 1992

—42 degrees

An occasion to celebrate—the return of the sun—yesterday at 2 P. M. it appeared from behind the peak on the high south ridge—and way visible for sixteen minutes. I was prepared.

Out came my hoarded can of seven-up, and from your good loaf I sawed a slice. It has been outside since it came, and frozen hard as wood. The crumbs were good too, so now it wouldn't be very long until there will be sun no end. Twin Lakes is a place where little things mean more: The return of the sun, the longest days, break-up, the longest day, blueberry time, the fall colors, the first snow at lake level, freeze-up, the shortest day, Thanksgiving, Christmas and the New Year. It is good to be here.

Thank you for all the good years. I still remember our first meeting. Again, wishing you girls the very best—and may 1992 be the best year ever. "God bless you kids," R. L. P.

P. S. Are you still taking pictures? Florence of the Mission Girls: More selective—must be worth the film.

Twin Lakes
July 28, 1992

Dear Doris and Florence,

It's a beautiful day at Twin Lakes. Cotton clouds, a green-white capping lake and the temperature near sixty. I'm up here at the point in Spikes cabin doing laundry and writing letters. My brother, Raymond, who arrived in his little yellow cub, is down at my cabin baking a loaf of sourdough bread and puttering around. I put him there to be close to his baby cub in case the wind comes strong up the lake. He has had a little experience with park porcupines rasping on the cabin logs, and a cow moose blocked out the big window she was so close to one morning. The city of Lynwood was never like that. July 4th is the day we flew in from Port Alsworth. I went out to help him get the floats ready to install.

A big community picnic the 4th, I saw many strange faces and lots of them. We were there again later, and as luck would have it, Babe and Mary came while we were there. Both looked real good, and Babe walks fast even at eighty-three years. He latched onto us and talked airplanes—same as years back. Last year, I heard that he said, "This is my last trip to Alaska." Guess Mary changed his mind. She would have to come put up fish.

I have thought of you kids so many times since your last nice care package came that I began to feel guilty about not writing. It has been a pretty busy ninety-two. Quite a few hikers and campers have come. *Alaska Wilderness Lodge* brings a beaver load of *One Man's Wilderness* fans occasionally, and along with them comes a big box from the Danish cooks they have at the lodge this year. They had General Norman Schwartzkopf for a guest and planned to fly him in. Then they learned I was at Port Alsworth. So, I missed getting his name in my guest book.

How has your year gone? Guess you never got to Nondalton or The Farm until now. Of course, you are acquainted with Lake Clark Air at Merrill Field. It is certainly a going outfit at the farm—four mechanics in that big new hanger—taking in outside work as well as keeping Lake Clark Air flying. Someone said they would have a crew of thirty this season.

Here, the big news is: "blueberries are as scares as hen's teeth." I have never seen such a poor showing. Sheep population is down drastically for

153

some unknown reason. Park Service did a second count, and it was no better than the first. My bunch across was sixteen, and should be about thirty. There were six new lambs instead of twelve to fifteen. Quite a few grizzly bears this past spring. I saw ten of which four were yearlings.

Sad news from Spokane, Spike C. ninety-one died May 28th, and quite suddenly—though he was in very poor health—went to sleep and didn't wake up. Did you know Frank B. who lived next to Port Alsworth and over where Chuck and Sara live? In recent years he lived at Big River, north of here—maybe a hundred miles. I heard a plane came to check on him, supply him, fly him out—or something, and he had passed away.

Now, I feel better that I have written these few lines. Now, the Mission Girls owe me a letter. Closing for now and wishing you girls the best of everything good.

Sincerely,

Dick Proenneke

Blueberries for pie, aguduk, or for the freezer if there are any left

TWIN LAKES
MARCH 9, 1993

—20 degrees—12:30 P.M. – Pretty Day

Dear Doris and Florence,

How come your letter doesn't come front and center now that I want to answer it? It must-a-got tucked in some other piece of mail.

It's nice out—nearly three inches of fluffy snow the last day or two, and One Man's Wilderness looks so white, it hurts the eyes. Lots of sun light now. The sun cleared another peak, and it is now light on my cabin from ten a.m. to 5:30 p.m.

I must stay close now, for Leon is due in any time. Part of the Port Alsworth Park Service was out attending school for three weeks, and due back this last week-end. Lee F. was to Georgia for two months of school, and he is due back, too. Thought Leon might be in today, tomorrow, next week or next month. Hope he hasn't forgot the eggs he said he would bring.

It has been a *sissy* winter since February 6th. It was minus fifty-five degrees the first day of February, and a minus thirty-four average temperature for the first six days.—and then a plus twenty-seven average for the rest of February. March is a little cooler. Last year, March had one minus forty-nine reading. April had a minus thirty degree. Guess it is true, *when the days begin to lengthen, the cold begins to strengthen.*

I haven't seen a sign of my resident wolf pack (ten) since early February. Leon reported Chuck H. seeing the pack near his homestead after they left here. Leon and I flew by alongside of them as they trailed along a mountain side. Some were black, and some nearly the size of ponies. I heard them howl one time since.

A wolverine was here about the cabin one night and a fox too. Some Ptarmigan feathers on the snow up Hope Creek—and yes, wolverine tracks and fox tracks too. My porcupine living under a big rock is gone too.

I still have my robbers three, and when do they start house-keeping? I must check my big bird book (900-page.) The great horned owl is a very early nester too.

Say! Your book, I enjoyed it—and of course wondered about some of the golden eagles' behavior and habits. I was to one eagle's nest on a ledge, but it was no more than one thousand foot above the lake, and the mist was not much. I did see a Goshawk young make its first solo flight—it hopped about the branches close to the nest, then stood on the edge facing out and looking. Suddenly it launched and flew about thirty feet to another tree. As they grow, they exercise their wings so they know they are strong enough. They nearly hover over the nest. And I can see males at six or ten thousand feet, but maybe in warm climates these are. A snake swallows its food whole, and young eagles are pretty large birds.

Sure do want to thank you for the Christmas treats—still working on them. That mystery morsel will be the last to go. I am curious, but am also patient. It does look interesting.

I remember you writing that Pete had surgery. Hope he is O. K. Hey, Leon, Linda, and Kate came, and so did Jay Hammond and Ranger Richard—lots of Company. Closing for now, hope all is well with you. Sincerely, Dick P.

Mama and Hatchlings

May 6, 1995

Bright and blowing, 46 degrees F.

Dear Doris and Florence,

"Surely tastes good to be back home again," but I like your home very much. I can just visualize you two having breakfast at the counter? I enjoyed your company and the round trip from Anchorage in the Olds 88—a very nice automobile. Thank you very much for the canned goods and the loaves of bread—the only bread I have for now. Clair and Liz have my sourdough starter, and it didn't meet the cub for the flight in. Next trip it will come. I could make biscuits of a sort but will wait. Had you sent more with me, Glen's Bonanza would have been over-loaded, and Leon's new cub (new for the Park Service) like your Olds, it is a late model and low time, blue and white. Last two numbers are 75 and Delta-modified baggage compartment that can be used for sleeping quarters.

A good flight to Port Alsworth. The airstrip is rough! Glen said. That was an invitation for me to smooth it before going to Twin Lakes. I pulled on an old pair of coveralls and had it one-third done by nine PM. Finished it and Ed P's road next day. Glen said we have lots of eggs; hens are laying like crazy, and the family eats lots of potatoes for we will have scads of spuds left over. Patty was down baby sitting with Menda. Leo, Menda's husband, was laid off and is working for Glenn this summer. They still have wind damaged airplanes waiting to be fixed.

Looks like Tony S. and Pat M. will become man and wife come late June. Tony asked me if they can honeymoon in Spike's cabin here close to me. I met her—nice and much younger than Tony. Glen has four Russian girls and two boys at present. Of course, Glen always cares about people.

Leon stuffed the cub and again, it was close. A nice smooth flight in. Dropped a heavy ice-testing rock which made a 3 to 4- inch cavity and lay 5 to 6 feet to the side. Landed, augured the ice to find it 30 inches. Candled all the way down, so it will go quickly. No robbers, but they came next morning and as tame as when I left them. They are nesting now. No robins, but I saw two at Port Alsworth. Ptarmigan are cackling on the mountain. Twenty sheep on the south slope across, very little snow there, and only patches here. No small birds here, but we saw ducks at the stream between the lakes. Leon said it snowed only a little after I left. I found two inches of water in the rain gauge, revealed at five this morning. Must not want these long days. Closing and wishing my Mission Girls the best of everything good. Sincerely, Dick

MAY 27–UPDATE

The pictures, Now I remember the contrast too great for the birds on snow. Go to manual and take a reading on something more the color of the birds. Perhaps your camera has the feature whereby you can hold a diaphragm setting by depressing the shutter release part way down, then take the picture of the birds on snow. Next winter, ok?

You have a lot of driveway to shovel—you don't, do you?

Nice pictures. Nice one of the trees and the lake. The treats are being appreciated. Half of the last loaf to go. Chunked and boiled the Alaska beet. Still ice in my under-the-spruce tree fridge. Lake ice about gone. Glen's ice is about gone. Glen is coming tomorrow to get me to grade runway and plant potatoes. Spring has been cool and more like the rainy season—in one shower, and that's a lot!!

My very best to you two. Thank you for the tour in your *Olds 88* and for the lunch. R.L.P.
Port Alsworth, Alaska

"John's House"
February 1, 1996

9:00 low overcast, calm and 25 degrees

Dear Doris and Florence,

Writing from the land where winter spends the summer. I think you must be enjoying it too. Ho Boy! Isn't it something? This morning's south 48 weather is some thing else. Folks down there wonder why I headed north in mid-December.

I enjoyed your letter and "Arctic Echoes" very much. By now I'm thinking a nice home has replaced the snowy status. The contractor never had it so good for building in winter. Not even a little more snow to move.

Just a little explaining on "John's House." Actually, it is John and Amy's house. They bought it from Rock and Linda who came from Minnesota to buy land and then build. John is a pilot for Alaska's Wilderness Lodge" at the narrows coming into Babe's Bay. Amy works at the lodge. I was holding down the fort for Clair R (Park Service) who was with Liz. When she went to the south 48 for a month, my cabin at Twin Lakes was frozen solid from the early cold spell.

John asked me to live in his house while he, Amy and their baby, along with two labs went to Seattle and California for a month. So, here I am half-way through their contract. Then I must go to Jay and Bella Hammonds for a few days. By then, the sun will be looking over the South mountains at my cabin. I hope lots of snow doesn't keep me here to clear the air strip. You probably know about Paul Carlson and his health problem. I see he and Irene most every day when I come by with their mail.

This home is very modern. The large rug makes me think of snowshoe season at Twin Lakes. It is so light in color and soft to walk on (no shoes please) and no screwdriver in your hip pocket when you sit in the big soft recliner. There are appliances I haven't touched. Clair and Liz are in Seward and Anchorage Park Service training for a few days, so I like to visit the up-lake of the village to check their heating system once a day. People say "don't go south, come to Port Alsworth and house sit for the winter." John's House is not far from Leon's and a very quiet location.

I would enjoy meeting Dr. Cates and his family. Perhaps, I will this summer. Several from past years threaten to come this summer.

I haven't flown over Twin Lakes, but Lee and Leon did early in winter. They report my cabin is as I left it. No break in by the black bear mom and cub. The heavy rains last fall did not cause flooding of Hope Creek, so my shinny bridge is still in place. The lake ice was 16 inches then and must be twice that now. Leon reported a pack of 20 wolves in the area. Just recently he saw a pack of 30 wolves in Lake Clark Pass. Caribou are many, but out of range, so the moose population will pay dearly. They reported very little snow there, and it is the same here at the present time. Maybe two inches here in the village. The airstrip has some ice, but very little snow. Weather report is "no snow in sight for the coming week end, but maybe next Monday."

I was at home in Primrose, Iowa from September 22 until December 17 when I flew north. Last time home was 1983 and 1976 was the last time I saw my brother Robert and his wife Dorothy (in Arlington, Virginia.) They are 85 and 86 now. My sister at home is 77, and Raymond the youngest is 74. Time marches on. I also have two other sisters, older than me. It was a rude awakening to go home and find everyone I knew Senior Citizens! One good friend my age walking with a cane; another with the early stages of Parkinson's disease.

I ask Sandy L. (Postmaster) what the population of Lake Clark Village is and was. A little surprised when she said, "75 full time." Mark is the electric meter reader. He says the number is 75. I was visiting chief ranger, Joe—farewell party a few evenings ago. Lots of new babies there. Little Dustin is growing tall. Sandy says he is nearly as tall as she.

Better close for now. Do hope this finds you two enjoying the best of health and good fortune. Sincerely, Dick

P.S. I enjoyed the snow bridge rescue story in "Guideposts."

PPS Please allow me to buy a few nails for your new home. RLP

Higher Ground

Anchorage, Alaska
PM March 6, 1998

Dear Doris and Florence,

Nice day and I have my snow shoveling caught up—my last day before flying to Port Alsworth (hopefully.) It's been such a long time, I thought I might put a short letter in your mail box. I have two addresses in my book, both the same. I'm sure the Postmaster is acquainted with *The Mission Girls* on a first-name basis. I get letters from Seattle with *R.L.P. 99653* for an address—no complaint 'til now.

I hope you girls have been happy and healthy since I heard from you last. I have traveled many miles since last first of October. I had planned to see all of my sisters and brothers one more time, and it is good that I did go, for we lost Robert (88) the senior of the 6. Earlier in February he was in the last stages of failing health, he and his wife Dorothy then living at their home in Arlington, Virginia. He was celebrating his birthday in early November, and I made it a point to be there, and from there to Iowa where sister Florence lives on the home place. She told me that she still gets *Our Daily Bread* thanks to you girls. Sister Helen and Lorene, both in their eighties, live in the area. I got the flu (Dec. 15) and pretty good! Turned to pneumonia and I was in no shape to fly. On the mend I went to Raymond's in Hemet, California to recuperate. Had a pretty thorough check-up. It ended with the recommendation that I take one Aspirin a day—pretty standard these days I believe.

Free to fly, so United said let's go to Anchorage March 3. Didn't take a half day, and here I was in Alaska once more. Good to be back! Tried to call Sis Clum a couple times today, but no answer. Christy, Glen's *Lake Clark Air faithful* at Merrill Field told me—and Sis wrote—that Babe has failed a lot recently. I am due to fly "Lake Clark Air" to Port Alsworth tomorrow at about 10 AM. Must call about 4 PM to be sure we fly. Glen is due to return from South America very soon or maybe he is home now. John S. of the John and Linda just arrived home from his mechanics job for the city. Linda will be home about six. Nice people. John's Mom and Dad are long-time Alaskans, and live in Seward. His Mom is 5 feet and ¾ inch tall.

I plan to stay at Port Alsworth until April and then go to Twin Lakes and stay until time to pull floats, at least. At Port Alsworth I will walk old Jenny, Mark and Sandy's black Lab, about 14 years and little Corky the Australian Terrier. Also, Muffin—Ed and Kathy Painters retriever. I sometimes walk Chewbacca—Lee and Shannon Fink's Golden retriever, the dog that swallowed a couple sox and it cost a thousand and more to have them taken out. And one more hiking partner, Sandy the Postmaster. She likes to go along and maybe lose a few pounds over time.

"Wait 'til after 3:30 pm and I will go, too" says she. Guess you know, Amber is getting married to Chris, one of Glen's mechanics. Dustin is going to school to become a doctor or a computer expert if the doctor plan doesn't materialize. Bet you girls know all of this, so sorry to have repeated what you know better than I.

So now One Man's Wilderness is due to come back. Time will tell. Enough rattling on, so I will call this enough and wish you girls the best of everything good. Wish we could butcher a pig with Babe one more time. Sincerely, Dick

Hemet, California
February 11, 2000

Bright and calm, 70 degrees F.

Dear Doris and Florence,

Surprised? I'm sure you must be. It has been a long, long time. I often thought I would *break the ice* but didn't get it done. Somewhere in my huge collection of mail I have your address—most sure I have. It was Sis who came to the rescue, saying she had forgotten to send it. Sis, you did send it quite some time back, and I—no I didn't lose it, just filed it too good!

You did write about your new home and sent a photo or two of it. I have heard of you two being stateside a time or two; that you stopped to see Vic in your travels. Those Terry and Vic days were good days, and the hog-butchering at Babe's was a highlight. I remember Doris suffering a blow to her head by a counter weight on our hoisting gear. Still sorry about that.

So now! How has life gone since you last heard from me? I have heard that you are still busy making the rounds checking on those in the hospital and care centers. Esther took me to see Babe one time when I was in Anchorage. She did all the visiting. I couldn't think of much to say to a totally silent Babe. If he could only talk a little bit it would help. No doubt you have seen him, and I think amazed at how good he looks. To me, he doesn't appear to be more than 70 years old if that, and he has gained weight. Again, if he could just talk a little bit. When I was house sitting for Clair and Liz at Port Alsworth—before he had his stroke, he would come at night to visit. I hesitated to let him go back alone, for it was icy. So, I would go back to Glen's with him. He insisted he could go alone, as he had a flashlight. Do you know I could very well be in the condition he is now—or worse—for I had a light stroke in Anchorage last mid-April. It got my left hand and memory pretty good.

I was at Twin Lakes before it happened; I awoke one morning and couldn't remember the call number to check in at headquarters. That was the sign that tried to tell me something, but I'd had a good summer and fall, with little trouble. Cutting wood was more work. Since my light stroke, I have made

173

a very good recovery. I am walking pretty good and my long-hand penmanship is better. I printed a few letters. I hope to return to Anchorage and Port Alsworth for a visit at least before the willow leaves unfold. I think you have heard that I signed my cabin over to the Park, and it was promptly declared a historical site, to be maintained by the National Park Service.

After forty treatments at Loma Linda Medical Center for prostate cancer, my brother Raymond is doing well, but living with the radiation side effects which may last for years. It is at his home here in Hemet, California that I am living. Summertime high was 110 degrees F. this last summer. A plus thirty has been our winter low.

You know that the book "One Man's Wilderness" came back after being out of print since about 1988. It is an attractive book and just recently it won the National best outdoor book award. And the new video "Frozen North" by Bob Swerer Productions in Ft. Collins, Colorado is my favorite I believe. Sis has one, so you can see the one-hour show when you are in Anchorage sometime. I wish Sis and Voight were more trouble free of seemingly minor health problems. A card just came from Daniel and wife at four-mile Tommy Creek Road,

Port Alsworth. It was post marked December 17th at Port Alsworth. The delay didn't happen in Sandy's Post Office. She is very good. Daniel's are a happy little family; she a true pioneer to spend so much time alone with little Daniel, Jr. while Daniel is in Anchorage Working in Voight's shop. David is doing very well with Alaska Airlines, but I think he would rather be Captain, flying out of Anchorage rather than L.A.

From home Sister Florence is going strong at 80 plus years. Helen and Larene (older) are having health problems.

This letter has gone on and on. Hope it is not boring. Closing for now and wishing you girls the best of health and good fortune. Please drop me a line sometime. I promise to answer promptly. Have a real good day. Dick.

Hemet, California
September 28, 2000

Dear Doris and Florence,

Just a note to say thanks for coming to Anchorage just so early to see me off, and for the box of good cookies to see me to Hemet. I saved one for brother Raymond. It was a good event-free flight, moderate turbulence for maybe 30 minutes out of Anchorage but smooth the remainder of the flight to Ontario where Raymond met me. Hemet pretty warm and it continued so for days and weeks. Today a high bright overcast and comfortably cool. The heat of summer is pretty well past.

I am wondering if you girls went to Port Alsworth for the video production by Bob Swerer, Sr. and Jr. from Fort Collins, Colorado. Sis was much in favor of a video of the community and its colorful residents. I do hope you made it, and saw ex-Governor Jay and Howard Bowman, plus more semi-old-timers.

Have you girls met Jana Walker, the Twin Lake's Ranger for the past three seasons? She came to Port Alsworth Park Service occasionally to do laundry, make phone calls and visit. She plans to visit us here in Hemet on her way to Arizona. About October 6th I saw Jay at Lake Clark Air in Anchorage. Not flying but looking for a plane to fly to Sandy's Post Office. When I saw him, he said he was looking for a bush rat older than he. I was that bush rat. He was doing pretty good with his new hip, but if I was FAA I would say Jay! You can fly solo, but only solo.

Our sister Larene back in Havana, Illinois Just got a new hip joint at Rochester, MN at 86 years, and is now home and on therapy. Florence is still going strong, Raymond is still living with his radiation side effects, but very slowly improving. Me, I am walking every morning and doing better but slowly. I trust you two are still the very active mission girls that I have known so many years. Did you ever get your new house paid for in full? If not, please let me help, OK?

Closing for now and wishing you the best of health and good fortune. My very best wishes, Dick.

P.S. Now I have your Wasilla address nailed down tight, so expect an answer if you write. OK?

Wasilla, Alaska
September 2000

Dear Dick,

This is a different computer program than we are used to, so will practice on letter to you. It was good to hear from you. Sorry we are so slow with an answer. We have had such a full summer and are STILL trying to catch up! (smile!)

We attended a birthday party for Betty's Grandson and enjoyed seeing a number of people we knew, including Norma J. The party was held at Wayne's house. Met one lady that looked familiar, and finally realized she was native of Naknek. Hadn't seen her since she was a little girl, forty years ago!

Glad to hear your flight went well. Nice of you to save one cookie for Ray. Though few, at least they were BIG. We should have brought more. Wonder what happened to the Video production. Their camera lens was broken?? Had we known we'd inquired of a friend who could possibly had the needed piece. No, we haven't met Jana. Do hope she was able to visit with you as planned. Glad you saw Jay.

Yesterday we had two visitors from Anchorage—originally of Pedro Bay. Carl and Margie Jensen. We made a big pot of Moose-Stew. Wish we could share some with you and Ray! Anyway, we have plenty left, and will have some for lunch. It was peppered more than usual, but it tasted fine to our company—and to us. Flo made a good batch of bread to go with it.

You ask about the house. We have been making extra monthly payments on the principal amount, hoping to *save money by paying it off sooner.* We are pretty disciplined with those payments! Our interest rate is 6.38, and it is a 30-year loan. Thanks for your very kind offer to help (almost made us cry!) The responsibility is ours, however, and we wouldn't want it on your shoulders. You will need your money for your future years. Only wish we could help YOU!! Thanks for being our friend all these years. Your letters and friendship mean a lot to us both. You have many friends here in Alaska—friends who respect and love you. We were grateful for the nice meal at Sis and Voight's place. It was fun. We also enjoyed meeting your Park Service friends when we picked you up in Anchorage. Hope to see them again.

Well, soup's on, so guess this letter comes to an end. Thanks again for taking time to write to us. We'll look forward to your next letter. Keep up those walks! Hi to Ray, too. Sincerely, Doris and Flo.

P.S. It was such a privilege to see Carl and Marje

HEMET, CALIFORNIA
OCTOBER 22, 2000

Sunday Cloudy Bright and Calm

Dear Doris and Florence,

Greetings from the sunny southwest. This weather is for my morning walk, but I feel a lot of locals see me and wonder at my sanity, for I hear the word chilly or nippy quite often. My morning chore after my walk is to pick up the magnolia leaves that fall during the night. Nights are usually dead calm. It is a small chore.

A letter came from Bob Swerer in Ft. Collins, CO. They did fly to Port Alsworth to do the video of the communities. They were able to hand-carry the big Sony Video Camera but mailed the camera Viewfinder with the Airlines. During the flight it was dropped hard and damaged beyond repair. Denver could get a replacement in Anchorage, but it would take longer than ten days. So, they cancelled the project and flew home to Ft. Collins. He didn't write that they will try again later. Sis will tell me of future plans, I'm sure. In his letter Bob wrote that he would phone soon, so we will hear of any future plans.

I did see Jay Hammond at Lake Clark Air—Merrill Field. He was walking with a cane and said, "If I fall, I can't get to my feet without something to hold to." No doubt he is doing much better now, for at that time his new hip was only a few months in use. He was looking for a small light plane to use for flight to Port Alsworth to get his mail. I am anxious to learn if he is flying again. I believe he does have a nephew who is a pilot and living with him and Bella.

Jana, the Twin Lakes Ranger, did come to visit. With her was a friend from Yosemite National Park. He is an electrician who has been at Yosemite for quite a long time. Jana has worked at Yosemite too, and will this winter. She wants to return to Twin Lakes next early June for her 4th season at Twin Lakes. She is a very capable ranger, and I am glad she is at Twin Lakes. She is also a hospital nurse but prefers to ranger in the summertime.

Because the mission girls are some of my favorite people, I would like to help them pay for that new house. So please accept my donation. Thanks again for the good cookies.

My Very Best to you Always, Dick

There is a river whose streams shall make glad the city of God.
Ps. 46:4

Be still, and know that I am God. I will be exalted among
the nations, I will be exalted in the earth.
Ps. 46:10

WASILLA, ALASKA
OCTOBER 29, 2000

Dear Dick,

Thanks for taking time to write to us giving us word on Jay. Thanks, too, for the explanation regarding Bob's viewfinder. We always appreciate hearing of friends—especially when we seldom see them.

Your $100 gift contribution towards our house left us with our mouths wide open. What can we say, not wanting to offend you by sending it back! We thank you!! Thank the Lord, too, for such a big-hearted friend! We certainly would never expect you nor anyone else to do this. We are placing the gift on the principal of the house. We humbly thank you.

Weather has been rather nice, with low-teen temperatures. We saw Northern Lights early this morning, and some bright twinkling stars. The sky darkened toward morning, then a nice sunrise with pink sky and mountains partially covered with snow.

Well, how is that for a Proenneke-style weather report? The week has been rather full, but we did manage to can about a dozen pints of salsa—from the last gleanings offered by Sis and Voight from their tomato plants! Will be nice for winter! We have plenty of canning jars, and can up as much garden or green-house produce available to us, or meat and salmon. Many people have been generous to us through years of time. May God bless them!!

Well, this is rather short, but need to mail letter now, lest we become overwhelmed with daily schedule. News says we may have light snow tomorrow (smile!) Sincerely, Doris and Flo.

Four volumes of the Journals of Richard L. Proenneke are available to the reading public.

More Readings From One Man's Wilderness, The Journals of Richard L. Proenneke, 1967. 1980. Published in 2005 by Lake Clark National Park and Preserve and edited by John Branson.

The Early Years, The Journals of Richard L. Proenneke, 1967-1973. Published by Alaska Geographic Association in 2010, ISBN 978-0-9825765-3-3, and edited by John Branson.

A Life in Full Stride, The Journals of Richard L. Proenneke, 1981-1985, Published by Friends of the Donnellson Public Library and the Richard Proenneke Museum, 2016, ISBN 978-168419714-9, AND EDITED BY John Branson.

Your Life Here is an Inspiration, the Journals of Richard L. Proenneke, 1886-1991 Published by the Friends of the Donnellson Public Library and The Richard Proenneke Museum 2018, ISBN 978-164316386-4, and edited by John Branson.